# Riley Unlikely

## WITH SIMPLE CHILDLIKE FAITH,

## AMAZING THINGS CAN HAPPEN

RILEY BANKS-SNYDER

*with* LISA VELTHOUSE

ZONDERVAN

*Riley Unlikely*
Copyright © 2016 by Riley Banks-Snyder

Requests for information should be addressed to:
Zondervan, *3900 Sparks Dr. SE, Grand Rapids, Michigan 49546*

ISBN 978-0-310-34787-3 (hardcover)
ISBN 978-0-310-34789-7 (international trade paper edition)
ISBN 978-0-310-34829-0 (audio)
ISBN 978-0-310-34788-0 (ebook)

Published in association with the literary agency of Brett Harris.

*Art direction: Curt Diepenhorst*
*Interior design: Denise Froehlich*

First printing in July 2016 / Printed in the United States of America

# Contents

# Riley Unlikely

This story is for the one who first wrote it.
He has written his love on my heart,
and it's my joy to share what a loving
and passionate Father he is.
And this story is for you.
It's my prayer that God will use this book
to reveal the love he's writing and
the story he's telling
in your life too.

# *Prologue:*
# AN UNLIKELY LOVE STORY

If anything has become clear to me over the past seven years, it's the link between love and craziness. It's what made me the head of a nonprofit organization by the time I was fourteen and transplanted me halfway around the world before I was twenty-one. You see, love makes you do crazy things. Like becoming a missionary to East Africa when you're in junior high, living away from all things typical teenager for months at a time, and falling in love with children who would become your own—so much so that you change the course of your whole life.

To be honest, Kenya and I were the unlikeliest pair. To someone with both a basic knowledge of Kenya and a basic knowledge of me, the mismatch would be fairly obvious. If it were up to me, I would go unnoticed in every crowd, everywhere, for all eternity, no question. In Kenya, my upbringing, skin color, and nationality make it almost impossible for me ever to blend in. And I'm probably one of the shiest people around, with what I consider to be a healthy dislike of public speaking. In rural Kenya, due to my being white, nearly everywhere I go a group gathers and I'm asked to make an impromptu speech or presentation. I get agitated every time I have to fly on a plane, so living an ocean away from my family and my hometown would be challenging even for a seasoned traveler. Plus, any familiarity I had with Swahili came from *The Lion King*, and I'm terrible at sleeping under mosquito netting.

It's a little crazy for a twelve-year-old American girl to plan a trip to Africa. It's a little wild for small-town American parents to support the plan wholeheartedly. And it's crazy wild to watch a small plan grow into something you wouldn't ever have thought to imagine: overseas trips for seven years running, a full-time nonprofit organization, outreach on two continents, and an improbable future.

Growing up I always dreamed of living in a big white house with a pretty green yard and white picket fence around it, filled with children. But now all I dream of is my beautiful home in Kenya with its tan and brown mud walls. It has a fence with a guard protecting it and a dirt-packed yard filled with dusty and giggling brown-faced Kenyan children, all calling this fair-skinned, brown-haired girl with the huge smile "Mama! Mama!"

Back when all this started, I never would have guessed that my family and I would be where we are today doing what we're doing. But apparently God likes to showcase his wild side. Thankfully, though, in this story God didn't reveal his wildness all at once. Instead, he unfolded things in spurts and pieces. Every small step of the way, he knew precisely how to move the plan forward without scaring me off completely. Sometimes he did that by forming important relationships out of seemingly random meetings. Sometimes he provided resources long before I could have known I would need them. And often he began changing my course long before I understood change was coming.

Possibly the best way to sum up this story is to highlight its unmistakable pattern. Year after year I've seen needs that seem impossible to meet, and year after year I've watched God meet them. Plenty of times I've gotten the sense that he's working things out with a wink and a grin so we're sure to appreciate the miracles. And more than once he's turned life as I anticipated it on its head, showing me that he can fill my aching heart in ways beyond my imagining. If I could have glimpsed the plan that God had in store for me and for us and for Kenya, I'm not sure I would have believed it. It probably would have seemed too huge, too complicated, and too masterful. I probably would have thought of myself as too young, too quiet, too average, or too inexperienced to be part of it.

So how did my life turn so drastically? Well, I have a long answer to that question. Everything started with a question, and then a trip, and then a stub of a pencil. I don't think I could have described it then, but I know now that God was using Kenya's kids to transform my heart. At the beginning, all I knew was that I wanted to help. I needed to help. And in looking at those children, I saw myself differently: they had what I lacked, and I had what they needed. I wanted to soak up their strength and revel in their contentment. I wanted to appreciate simple joys like they did. And although I had never thought of myself as materially rich, I could see through their eyes that I am.

This is the story of how God took a thirteen-year-old girl and transformed her into a twenty-year-old missionary. It's the story of how he can take seemingly mismatched parts and fit them together brilliantly. It's the story of how he can change our lives and dramatically shift our dreams. All this time, he has been tailor-making me for Kenya's kids, and them for me: a perfect match from an unlikely love story.

CHAPTER 1

# Swinging Doors and
## *Sacrifices*

Waking up on March 16, 2010, I had butterflies in my stomach and ants in my pants, nervous and excited about the adventure awaiting me. I was dressed and ready to go long before my dad and probably looked like a new pup sitting at the door with her leash in her mouth, only instead of the leash, I was surrounded by suitcases busting at the seams with new toys ready to be played with.

Today I would be leaving my own country for the journey of a lifetime. I had just become a teenager, and I'd had big dreams for a while now.

The year before, I'd found out that my aunt and uncle and baby cousin were moving to Kenya. My uncle Logan, my dad's younger brother, and my aunt Julie had been considering the possibility of short-term mission service and had been keeping their ears to the ground about opportunities that might be a good fit for their family. Specifically, they had been looking for a place where they could both be of service and Uncle Logan's training as a family physician could be put to good use.

Shortly after baby Liam was born, they had found a place: Tenwek, a mission hospital in a village called Bomet, in West

Kenya. Tenwek had been established eighty years before as a place that would demonstrate God's love by providing affordable, often free, health care services in the region. In its early days, the hospital delivered babies, dispensed medicine, and offered general health care. These days Tenwek is a whole complex of buildings that provides everything from dental and basic lab work to ob-gyn, surgical, and emergency care. It also has a certified nursing school and a medical internship program.

The hospital relies mostly on a stream of medically trained Christian missionaries—doctors, nurses, technicians, and others, many of whom moved an entire family unit to Kenya for several months or more, living just down the hill from the complex and giving of their skills and expertise full-time while earning zero income. Family members were another vital part of Tenwek's mission. Many of them filled administrative and supportive roles at the hospital, but more than that, they all lived in the local community of Bomet. In their daily village interactions, they could reach out and put God's love on display.

Tenwek fit the criteria Uncle Logan and Aunt Julie had been seeking. This amazing opportunity would require an enormous commitment, and my uncle and aunt were about to take it on. In just a few months, they would take off for Wichita, Kansas, to complete six months of training, and then they would be in Africa!

It was an exciting time for the Banks family. We were thrilled for Logan and Julie and eager to see what God would do in and through them. Many of us were learning East Africa trivia to be better informed about the place where they would be living and serving. I began doing a little informal research myself. I checked out the Tenwek website and perused online photo albums of the area. I read up on the average household income of a family in Kenya and tried to figure out how different it was from the United States. I searched for stories about East African kids and their

Left to right: Dad, me, Aunt Julie, and Uncle Logan Banks

schools, hoping to understand a bit of what life was like for other kids in the region.

Logan and Julie's plan to live and serve in Africa fascinated me. The idea that a young family could pick up and move to another country, simply to serve others and introduce them to Jesus was, for me, a revelation, even though I had spent my childhood growing up in a Christian family and in church. (Apparently I hadn't been especially great at paying attention.) But I had caught on—better late than never, I guess—and had become intrigued by what my uncle and aunt would be doing half a world away. Eventually, all my research added up to one wild idea: I wanted to see it all for myself.

To be clear, my desire to go stemmed from both family and missions—probably a 50/50 split. I thought it was pretty neat that Kenya could potentially combine both those things for me. If visiting my family meant I could have a chance to play some small role in the mission field, why wouldn't I go? If doing mission work in Kenya gave me a chance to serve side by side with my family, what could be better than that?

But there was one glaring problem: when you're twelve, being hooked on a trip to another continent doesn't mean anything unless you have permission.

This will probably tell you a lot about how my family works: When I first asked for permission to go to Africa, I didn't think the moment required any fanfare, such as a serious discussion, or even the presence of both parents. I was riding in the car one day while my mom was running errands, and I simply brought up the subject and asked.

"Mom, when Uncle Logan and Aunt Julie are in Kenya, do you think I could go visit them and help out?"

My mom's eyes got wide and her eyebrows shot up. She stayed quiet for a while, and when she eventually spoke, I could tell she was being cautious with her words. They were drawn out and enunciated carefully.

"I don't see . . . why . . . you *shouldn't* . . . go."

This will probably tell you a lot about me: I took that as a yes.

Back at home that evening, I was eager to get my dad up to speed. I knew that for me to go to Africa, I'd need one of my parents to play chaperone, and I figured Dad was my best bet. He too was fascinated about Logan and Julie's adventure since first hearing about it, so I was hoping that as he pondered the possibility of getting involved, he'd be willing to add me to the equation.

So I asked. And he was. He was!

That night, as my two younger brothers crashed around the house and played video games, my mom, dad, and I sat in the living room and began talking logistics. None of us had ever planned a trip like the one we were considering, and we had a lot of questions.

*How expensive would it be?*

*How would we pay for the flights, passport fees, and other travel costs?*

*Would it be safe?*

*When would be a good time to go?*

*What would we do there if we actually did make the trip?*

Questions in hand, we did some more research. We started by talking with Logan and Julie about volunteer possibilities, travel specifics, lodging, and whether my age might limit what we could do. All their responses were encouraging. We would have plenty to do and numerous opportunities to help, they said. Plus, they could help us get around in Kenya and we could stay with them at their place.

The more we talked, thought, and prayed, the more excited we all became. It never seemed like God was closing any doors on our idea; instead, he kept swinging them open wide. We began sketching out a possible plan and an estimated budget. We figured that Dad and I could go for two weeks around the time of my spring break so I wouldn't miss too much school. We could visit Logan, Julie, and Liam, soak up some of the local culture, and serve wherever we were needed. It would be fantastic!

And it would be expensive. My dad and I would need money for international flights, some overnight stays, meals, passport fees, road transportation, and probably a few unplanned incidentals. Our estimated grand total was about $5,000.

My parents made it clear from the start that paying for a trip to Africa was going to take faith. We would have to trust that God could supply whatever amount we needed in order to go. We knew from the Bible that God owns the cattle on a thousand hills— everything belongs to him. Although we had no idea how God might supply for my dad and me, we knew that if he wanted us in East Africa, he would somehow come through.

But we had to make some sacrifices too. Sacrifice had been a specific mandate, in fact. In giving me permission to go to Kenya, my parents had made a deal with me: they would help pay for my trip if I would agree to forfeit Christmas gifts and unnecessary purchases for the year. As far as I could tell, swapping some presents for a trip to Africa was a no-brainer. I happily accepted the terms and set my sights on following through.

# CHAPTER 2

# IT TAKES A
## *Village*

If it had been up to me, I wouldn't have sent out a letter asking friends and family members for financial support. I knew that was something missionaries do, and although I figured it was a great thing for them, I didn't think of my dad and me as being in that category. We were going to Kenya for such a short time, and part of our trip's purpose was to visit family members who actually *were* missionaries. Why would other people want to help us do *that*?

"I just don't think anybody would send us money," I explained to my best friend, Kassadee. I assured her that a support letter would be a giant waste of time and effort.

But Kassadee wasn't so pessimistic. "You really don't think anybody would want to chip in?"

I shook my head. I might have even twisted up my face a little. To me the idea of asking others to contribute money had one inevitable outcome: zero.

Kassadee wasn't convinced, however, and she pressed the issue. "You know," she said, "stamps don't cost much, and you might be surprised. I'll bet some people would be excited about the chance to help you make this dream come true."

In other words, *What could it hurt to ask?*

The process turned out to be fairly straightforward: Dad and I explained how we planned to visit family and serve in Kenya, shared an estimate of how much our trip would cost, and asked for prayers and financial help to get there. We sent out the letter to our family members and a few close friends, and then we waited to see whether anybody would reply.

The response was overwhelming. And it just kept getting better.

I've mentioned that I'm pretty quiet and like to stay in the background of things. For example, I've never loved the idea of having a birthday party. I just don't like to be the center of attention. But with our trip on the books and my thirteenth birthday on the horizon, even I could agree that a special shindig was in order.

So, just before our trip, my parents invited all my friends to come over and celebrate, on one condition: they couldn't bring any gifts for me. Instead, each girl agreed to bring a small toy or toys for kids in Kenya. I could load the gifts into my suitcases and distribute them on behalf of all of us.

It was one of the best parties I've ever been to! All of us were happy because we knew the gifts were earmarked for kids who had barely anything. As I opened them one by one—a soccer ball, a mini bowling set, some Matchbox cars—we all gushed. Everybody seemed overjoyed to be able to give.

At that point our family had been gearing up for Kenya for nearly a year, and that whole time, others had been gearing up with us. They had prayed, they had contributed funds, they had surprised us, they had celebrated with us. God had used each one of them to pull us along, strengthening our belief that we were on the right track.

That's why when Dad and I took off at last, it felt like more than just the two of us were making the trip. We carried with us the eagerness and faith of many others. Because of God's work through them, the plane tickets in our names had been fully paid for and our suitcases were stuffed with great toys. Our hearts were brimming with excitement. I felt like I had already been on a whirl of an adventure, and the trip had only just begun.

# CHAPTER 3

# Culture
## *Shock*

My mom had cried when she left Dad and me at the airport. I knew she was sad that we were going to be separated; that was part of it. But mostly I could tell she was uneasy. Dad and I were going to a place where nearly everything would be unfamiliar, and between the two of us, our international travel experience amounted to one trip, when Dad and Mom took a vacation to Mexico. Plus, one of us was barely a teenager.

Speaking for the thirteen-year-old, though, I hadn't felt many pretravel jitters. Even crossing the Atlantic and then jumping the Mediterranean wasn't freaking me out as much as it normally would. The promise of Kenya was too exciting! That's why it was particularly ironic that I got uncomfortable when I did, which wasn't until we *stopped* flying. Our arrival in Nairobi was the part that first rattled me.

As the plane touched down, I peered out the window and scanned from left to right. I thought I would see desert grasslands and maybe a few giraffes. But where I had expected a safari post-card scene, I found big-city commotion and plenty of green. There was no shortage of thick shrubs, leafy trees, and towering palms in Kenya's capital. Wide patches of ground were covered with grass too; it was nothing like the dry, uninhabited countryside I had anticipated. The downtown skyline was visible from the airport, and from that perspective, Nairobi looked like any other metropolis. From what I could tell, it just as easily could have been Dallas or Cincinnati.

We hadn't even left the tarmac yet, and already it was clear to me that this was not the Africa I had pictured. That Africa was more rural, more arid, and far less developed: erase the buildings, highways, and dense population, and replace all of it with footpaths, scrub brush, and chalky, reddish dirt. (Apparently what I lacked in geographical awareness I had more than made up for in stereotypes.) Right off the bat, I could see that my basic assumptions about Kenya needed to be recalibrated. But before I could even begin to process reality, the plane's door opened and foul air rushed in.

Addressing cultural differences related to certain types of smells will probably never be appropriate, but here goes. In the United States it's not entirely uncommon to smell body odor, but it's fairly unusual to smell body odor that has soured. By contrast, in Kenya the smell of sour body odor is practically everywhere. It was day one, hour one in Africa, and at least one of my five senses was under assault.

Uncle Logan had arranged to pick us up from the airport, outside of customs. Almost nothing had changed about him, but the context was so different that for a moment it seemed like everything had shifted. Suddenly Uncle Logan wasn't just a taller, bearded version of my dad; in Nairobi he had become White Uncle Logan—the only light-colored face in the crowd. I knew that if he stuck out that much because of his skin color, I would stick out that much too.

The drive from Nairobi to Bomet took three and a half hours. The majority of our drive was on a highway that cuts through the middle of the Great Rift Valley in Africa's Great Lakes region, just north of the Serengeti plain. The landscape was stunning; the whole valley was a lush green from the rainy season, and we could see mountains in the distance, a wide blue sky, rolling hills, and low, sprawling trees. But the natural wonders all around us weren't the only sights to take in. There were cities and towns, trucks hauling loads one way or another, people traveling, even donkeys pulling a cart—all set against a backdrop of vibrant, brightly colored paint.

Most buildings in Kenya are constructed with cement blocks and rebar or wood and corrugated tin. After a building's walls go up, typically no facade is added. Instead, many buildings simply get a coat of paint, and they become their own billboard. It wasn't uncommon to see a whole store or food stall hand-painted into an advertisement: slogans, logos, sponsored products—you name it. As a marketing strategy, it definitely worked.

Overlooking the town was Tenwek Hospital, an open-air complex comprised of various medical buildings. Down the hill from there, a row of apartments had been built for the hospital's volunteer staff. We pulled up in front of one of them, and Uncle Logan, Dad, and I spilled out. We were immediately greeted by Aunt Julie's vibrant smile. Liam was on her hip, his blond hair catching the light. Three months of growing had changed the baby a lot.

"You're here! Welcome! Come in, come in!"

After giving us a quick tour of their home, Aunt Julie showed Dad to his room and me to mine. She and I had barely walked through the door of my bedroom when some kids outside popped their heads up and peeked in through the window. Seeing their faces there so suddenly surprised me, but Aunt Julie wasn't fazed. She smiled at the kids, then grabbed a curtain and pulled it over the window.

"They'll never leave otherwise," she explained with a shrug.

Left alone in my bedroom, I unzipped my suitcase and unpacked some of my things. Dad and I hadn't brought much clothing or many personal things because we had wanted to reserve most of our baggage space for items that could be shared with Kenyan kids and their families. I felt a surge of excitement to think that we could finally give away the toys and little games we had been collecting for months!

Back in the living room, I saw a bunch more kids outside the window. It wasn't tough to guess whether these kids were poor. From what I had seen of Bomet, most of the locals were poor. The hospital apartments obviously had been built for doctors visiting from first world countries. Logan and Julie's had four bedrooms, one full bathroom, a typical Western kitchen, and even a fireplace. But those apartments were far from standard; in fact, they were massive and seemed out of place. Just around the corner from us, whole families were living in tin-roofed, one-room cement

PLAYING WITH CHILDREN ON TENWEK CAMPUS

structures. For the most part, that was the flavor of the neighborhood. It was no wonder, then, that the local kids hung around and tried to sneak peeks into the apartments. The inhabitants were rich outsiders, exotic and interesting to observe.

The boys and girls saw me standing at the living room window. Immediately a few of them ran over and started doing silly dances in front of me. I played along, hiding behind the furniture and then jumping out suddenly. The kids laughed and then danced some more. I laughed and then jumped out again. We kept up that pattern for a while, until finally I asked my dad and Uncle Logan if I could go outside to play in person. With their permission, I grabbed some brand-new jump ropes from my suitcase and rushed outside.

The kids and I played all day until sunset, jumping rope and making up games. Somehow during that time, the Kenyan kids turned me into a lion. I never figured out why; maybe because I was bigger and lighter colored than all the other kids. I was happy to go along with it. I put on my best lion roar and chased them around for hours.

That night I went to bed eight thousand miles away from home, and in many ways that distance couldn't possibly have felt more apparent. My body couldn't seem to figure out what time zone it was in, and my light skin felt strange among so many dark people. The poverty I had seen was unsettling, and the language barrier had been a constant challenge already. So far Africa had been mostly *not* what I had expected, and I felt like I had repeatedly lost my bearings already. But I was here! In Kenya! God had brought my dad and me almost halfway around the planet, and he had supplied everything we needed to make the trip. If he could do that so easily, then surely he could also help me adapt quickly.

I could hardly sleep that night, tired as I was, for all my excitement. I couldn't wait to see what the next day would hold.

# CHAPTER 4

# Bin Beds

## FOR BABIES

There is a common Swahili word for "white person" in Kenya: *mzungu* (m-ZUHN-goo). This word has a colorful legend attached to it.

Depending on who you ask, you might hear that the literal translation of *mzungu* is simply "white person." Or you might be told that the meaning of the word is tied to a centuries-old narrative, in which case you would hear a different definition. As the story goes, when European settlers first arrived in Africa, they were known for their inability to find their way around. These people were so often lost on the continent that their lostness came to define them. Before long the nickname *mzungu* just seemed to fit. According to this version, the word means "aimless wanderer" in one regional dialect, and it sounds a lot like "spinning in one place" in another.

With the "lost" legend in mind, some people would probably tell you that *mzungu* is a racial slur or an insult. I don't know whether that's true or not, and I also couldn't tell you whether the tale of the disoriented European settlers is fact or fiction. What I can say is this: mentally and emotionally I was so disoriented that the idea of "white person" becoming synonymous with "lost" in Africa was easy for me to believe.

Shortly after Dad and I arrived in Bomet, I was about to spend my first day volunteering at Tenwek. Aunt Julie and I were going to help with infant feeding in the neonatal unit, and I was so giddy with excitement about it that I skipped breakfast.

It was still early morning when Julie and I made our way to the hospital complex. The road from the apartment was a rocky uphill climb, and our progress was slow and a little restricted. In Bomet and many other parts of Kenya, it's considered inappropriate for a woman to show her legs; pants and shorts are seen as provocative, and even slightly fitted skirts are socially off-limits. Julie and I were both wearing ankle-length dresses with T-shirts underneath. In other words, we each had a hem that limited our steps and two layers overheating our torsos. Back in Branson, when I had shopped for clothes that would adequately cover my legs in Kenya, dresses had been on sale. Had I understood at the time how hot Kenya gets and how active I would be, I gladly would have spent a few extra dollars to avoid doubling up on fabric. I soon learned that loose fitting skirts and T-shirts were the way to go!

When Aunt Julie and I arrived at the hospital complex, I was relieved to see that the building was open-air. Under the shade of a roof, with windows vented, we would at least be out of the sun and have a chance for a breeze. But no sooner had I finished telling myself this, than we made our way to the neonatal unit and found it to be tightly sealed. For the safety of new babies, the unit was kept sterile: no propped door, no windows venting, no breeze.

"Here we go," Julie said, smiling. She opened the door, and we walked inside.

She was used to the heat, the sights, and the smells inside that room—which is probably why she didn't warn me about them. They hit me like a blast. The room was small, no bigger than the average American living room. In it were seven or eight babies, and each of them was lying in a medium-sized, clear plastic storage tub. In the United States those bins would have been used to store craft supplies, but here they were cradles. All the babies were sleeping naked, with no diapers, so they were soiling themselves and the bins.

The bare plastic was off-putting to me, but I had to admit it was sensible under the circumstances. The upside to plastic beds was that they wipe down in no time. For some people, that is.

Part of our job was to clean the babies. A handful of Kenyan mothers showed up that morning too. Each of them went straight to her baby and got started, while a couple of nurses assigned the remaining babies to the other volunteers, including Aunt Julie and me.

"Miss"—a nurse gestured my way, then motioned toward a plastic tub in the center of the room—"you take this one, please. The mother is being treated for mental health issues."

Lying inside the container was a tiny, skinny, sound-asleep baby girl. She had a short crop of curly black hair, and she was so new that her skin was still fairly light in color. Also, apparently her bowels were functioning properly. This girl was going to need a very good cleaning. She was motherless for the day, and I was the stand-in, so I wanted her to have the best I could give. I grabbed some towels and a little water and went to work.

My tiny, sweet girl was so bare and so dirty. A dense, foul odor emanated from her "crib." At some level I knew there was nothing inherently wrong with those things—Kenya was just hotter than Missouri, the Kenyan approach to diapering was just different, and rural African baby care just had fewer frills than I was used to. But while cognitively I knew the baby was okay, I couldn't get myself to *feel* okay about her circumstances. Instead, I kept thinking my girl belonged in a sheet-lined bassinet or a pink-trimmed cradle. She needed a diaper, a cute onesie, a hand-knitted hat and booties, and a room that smelled fresh and clean. Didn't she?

The way of life that made sense to me was half a world away. By comparison, the place where I stood was strange and unsettling. It was throwing new, confusing customs at me faster than I could process them, and tunnel vision had kicked in as a result. I was losing track of my head. I was about to lose my grip too.

As time passed, the Kenyan mothers washed their babies confidently, like it took almost no effort at all. Holding their infants in one hand and a damp cloth in the other, they turned and flipped the wiggling babies easily. They didn't seem one bit worried about dropping the kids or getting smeared by something gross. They finished the task quickly.

I, on the other hand, was not even halfway done. My skin felt slippery with sweat, and it seemed highly possible that a day-old baby could slide right out of my hands and onto the floor. If not that, then there was at least a good chance I'd end up streaked with feces. My stomach churned just thinking about it. *Disgusting.*

I knew that connecting a word like that with a sleeping infant was terrible, and although I wanted to stop, I kept doing it anyway. On one hand, that baby's tiny pucker of a mouth and her contented expression had absolutely melted my thirteen-year-old heart. I was watching her face intently, tuned in to every hint of a whine or wince, prepared to jump in response to her needs. On the other hand, the whole time I was cleaning her, over and over I was thinking, *Nasty. Ew.*

As the Kenyan mothers finished their cleanings, one by one they took a seat on a row of short, wooden stools lining the far wall. Then, facing the center of the unit, each woman began feeding her child. Because the room was small and because the lone living beings in the middle of it were my baby and me, the women were looking directly at us. And we were putting on quite a spectacle.

Not only was I nearly a decade younger and multiple shades lighter, but I was also fanning myself and wiping away sweat constantly. My awkward, hesitant approach to baby cleanup was like a flashing sign to any and all observers: "This one's uncomfortable!" It was almost as if I were *trying* to be the sore thumb, sticking out like crazy.

On that day, in that little room, there was no way I could have blended in with those Kenyan mothers, no matter how hard I might have tried. They were everything I wasn't: grown, strong, dark, and in the know. I was a minority in every way: young, white, foreign, and clueless. Their skin glistened with sweat just like mine did, but the heat didn't seem to faze them. Tenwek's baby-care customs (smells and bare bottoms included) weren't throwing them off at all.

With a few more tentative wipes of skin and plastic, my baby and I managed to complete her cleaning. I swaddled her up, breathed a long sigh of relief, and prepared myself for the easy part: feeding. How difficult could it be? The task seemed so straightforward that I wasn't even taking the question seriously. Looking back, I should have.

Two elements are particularly helpful in the feeding of a newborn. I know that now because in the neonatal unit I didn't have either of them. The elements are (1) a bottle and (2) a wakeful baby. The only feeding tools on hand were small plastic medicine cups, the kind that come on top of a bottle of cough syrup. Carrying a few ounces of milk in one of these back to my girl's plastic bin, I stood motionless for a moment, bewildered. My baby was still asleep, her lips pressed delicately together. It was an adorable, restful pout, but I knew I was going to have to interrupt it if I wanted her to eat.

I began attempting to wake her by trying out the prime tickling zones: her belly, her sides, under her armpits, under her chin.

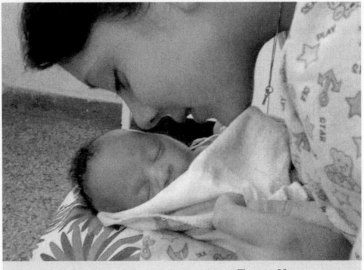

ME WITH ONE OF THE PREEMIE TRIPLETS AT TENWEK HOSPITAL

None of them seemed to register; she dozed on. Next I bounced her lightly and scrunched up my nose against her cheek. I tickled around to the base of her back and then tried the soles of her feet. I traced her jawline, her nose, and her lips with my fingers. I patted her bottom and poked behind her knees. I hoisted her into the air and jostled her a little, letting her legs dangle and swing. Still nothing. I knew that a tiny, baby-sized jolt of discomfort was what she needed—some harder squeezes on her arms maybe, or perhaps a little more pressure when tickling her feet—but I felt firmly set against it. This girl was brand-new, she was all alone, and there was no telling when her mother would be able to come back to her. It seemed important to protect her from additional traumas, even the smallest kinds.

I continued with bounces, pats, tickles, jostles, and dangles, but my baby wasn't responding to any of it. Then all that changed. From across the room, one of the nurses noticed that my baby wasn't eating, and she decided to take matters into her own hands.

She strode over to where we were, picked up the medicine cup of milk, and pinched my little girl's cheeks, hard. My baby squirmed and squealed, and as her mouth opened with sound, the nurse poured a small stream of milk into the center of it.

My girl's sleepy eyes opened. She gurgled and coughed. Then she swallowed and let out a sharp cry. The nurse handed me the medicine cup, nodded helpfully, and smiled. "You can do it like that," she said.

As the nurse walked away, I immediately gave my girl a protective snuggle and looked into her face. No surprise, she was already getting back to her snoozing—except this time something was different. Her bottom lip was protruding, and seeing that reaction was all it took for a fiery, stubborn impulse to spark in me. I did not like that one of my baby's features had turned sad.

I moved my face closer to hers. "That hurt, didn't it?" I whispered. I was determined that for as long as I was on shift, no more pinches would be necessary. I perched the rim of the medicine cup above her lips and squeezed it to form a spout. A couple of times my baby's lips opened long enough for me to pour in some drops. Other times she puckered them back together so quickly that the milk dribbled down her cheek and into her swaddle blanket instead. Most of the time she didn't open her mouth at all.

My right arm began cramping from holding the cup in the air. My left arm was already sore from holding the baby, and my legs were starting to burn and ache from all the bouncing. The room wasn't getting any cooler, and its wafting aromas were still overpowering.

Suddenly the colors in the room started to fade. People and objects were turning grainy, like an old photo. My head was feeling airy, and my body was getting awkward and dizzy.

The room started to spin. Instinctively I put the baby back in her bin, then made my way, one unsteady foot after the other, toward the door that led outside. It took a supreme effort to keep from hitting the floor.

There was a little wooden bench outside, and I sat down heavily. *Get horizontal so you don't faint*, I told myself. Intending to use the bench as a bed, I lowered my body onto the seat. Then everything went black.

When I came to on that bench, I was mortified. I was supposed to be taking care of someone else's baby. I was supposed to be an asset to the hospital staff, an aid to their work. Instead, I'd let them down. Not only did I have to sideline myself and go recoup, but I also stole Aunt Julie away from her volunteer work. She held my arm while I walked, weakly and woozily, back to her apartment and into bed.

I slept a long time. When I woke up, I tried to process things. Before that spell, I had fainted a number of times back home for no apparent reason. Although my medical practitioners hadn't been able to figure out why I was fainting so much, one of my doctors had taught me how to avoid it in the future. With practice, I had become pretty good at his method. I could usually identify the warning signs and halt the process midway. The fact that I passed out in Kenya, despite all I had already learned about fainting, caused me to think a little longer and harder about how I was doing there. On the day I fainted, sure, I had skipped breakfast, and yes, Tenwek was brutally hot—but was there more to it? I began to suspect there was.

Even after having chilled out with some rest and some food, I couldn't shake a particular agitated feeling. I still felt confused and discombobulated. My reactions seemed unpredictable and awkward. My thoughts were contradicting themselves, and my emotions were unreasonably out of sync. Everything was scrambled. I had been away from home for only one day and already I felt lost in Kenya.

# CHAPTER 5

# Masop

After that first day at Tenwek, my dad and I spent a few more nights at Uncle Logan and Aunt Julie's apartment. I helped with some cooking, Liam care, and cleaning. I also played with the neighborhood kids some more and volunteered at the neonatal unit again—more successfully! In other words, I split my time: part in a big home built for Western doctors, part hanging out and serving in slums. The differences between the two lifestyles were shocking.

When I was in the apartment with plenty of food and typical American comforts, I felt at home. At the same time, feeling at home didn't seem right anymore, considering the poverty people were living in just around the block.

*Why do I like having so much?*

*Why should I have so much when others have so little?*

*Why am I not giving* more *away?*

But by the same token, there were times when it seemed almost discouraging to give. The poverty and need around us ran so deep that some days I wondered whether any help could make a lasting impact.

*Does any of this really do any good?*

*Are we just slapping Band-Aids on a gushing wound?*

*Is the problem too big, or could giving more actually change things?*

My time in Kenya was churning up more questions than

answers, and it had me ping-ponging between conflicting emotions. This was especially true midway through our trip, when my dad and I went on a very expensive preplanned weekend safari. I couldn't help but feel guilty about the price tag. When nearly everyone around you is lacking basic necessities, it feels selfish and a little disgusting to have any extras for yourself. So when we checked in for the weekend, despite our excitement for the adventure ahead, something about it already felt sour.

We stayed for a few nights in tents that were five-star rated. We had three delicious meals served daily and access to a pool for relaxing and swimming. During the day, we piled into Jeeps to see vast expanses of open land, not to mention giraffes, antelope, monkeys, and rhinos in the wild. At night we heard hippos fighting in the river. The beauty of our surroundings seemed nothing but exotic, and we were experiencing all kinds of new facets of God's creativity.

But we were tourists, traveling in clean, untorn clothes and carrying gear that was in good condition. Our stomachs stayed full, and the reality of Kenya's poverty stayed outside the perimeter of our daily expeditions. Most people on our tour might have been surprised to discover how much of a luxury this safari was compared to the way Kenyans were living just a couple of towns over. Staying ignorant about it all would have been fairly easy. But I had held babies at Tenwek, and I had played with kids in the streets of Bomet. For me, forgetting the difference was impossible.

I wondered, *How might things be different if people in the West knew how rich and privileged most of us are? Why is it so easy for us to stay ignorant instead?*

When our safari was over, Dad and I returned to Bomet briefly; then it was time for the next phase of our work. We packed a couple of bags and hired a car and driver. Then, one afternoon while Uncle Logan was at the hospital, Aunt Julie and baby Liam rode with us across town. Mosop School and Orphanage was just a quick jaunt from the apartment, but when we got there it felt like it was worlds away.

We arrived during class time and were met by the headmaster and his wife, who together had founded and also ran the school. They introduced us to two young American women, Raika and Kaitlyn. They were college students working in Bomet for course credit that semester, and they had arrived at Mosop the day before. As a group, Raika and Kaitlyn, Aunt Julie and Liam, and Dad and I were led to a common area outside because our appearance was about to trigger a school assembly.

The headmaster addressed the group.

"Good morning," he said. "Today we have some special guests from the United States. Listen to them now, because they have important messages to share with you."

Apparently this was the common practice in rural areas of Kenya. When you are white and American in rural Kenya, it is generally assumed that you are exceptionally educated and wildly rich, and that you have something worthwhile to say. In other words, you have highly valued commodities—namely, education and funds—that can be passed on. Whether you're the president of a country or just some thirteen-year-old in town to visit family, if you're *mzungu*, then you're usually treated almost as if you're royalty. And that includes quickly being expected to make a speech.

My dad came up with something on the spot. Raika and Kaitlyn did too. (I learned later that because of their work in Kenyan schools that summer, they were used to giving impromptu speeches.) As for me, I would have sooner crawled into a hole than talk to an entire student body, especially on no notice. So I smiled, gave a little wave, and simply said, "Hi, I'm Riley. I'm really glad to be here."

When the speeches and presentations were over, the headmaster dismissed the assembly so we could all have a little free time. We spent the rest of the school day playing with the kids and getting to know them. My dad hung out with the secondary school boys; there were some old tires on the school grounds, and Dad wanted to find some rope and teach them how to rig up a tire swing with it. The secondary school girls had flocked to Raika and Kaitlyn, and together they were all chatting away. I stayed with the primary school students, playing Red Light, Green Light and trying hard to figure out who was who as the kids ran past me.

We were having so much fun, I didn't want it to stop. But I also couldn't wait to leave, because I knew when I left the school for the evening I would be able to open my suitcase and dig out the rest of the toys that Dad and I had brought with us from the States. Many of the Mosop kids weren't even wearing shoes, so I guessed they would enjoy opening a small gift that would be just for them. Giving toys to these great kids was going to be an absolute delight.

Later in the afternoon, Aunt Julie and baby Liam took off with the driver so they could return to their Tenwek apartment. Dad and I were going to remain at Mosop for four nights, volunteering at the school and staying with the headmaster and headmistress in their home.

The house was also an orphanage for about ten local children. In rural Kenyan culture, it's not uncommon for children to lose their parents to AIDS, water-borne diseases, complications from childbirth, or other health-related causes. It's also not uncommon for parents to abandon their children. Sometimes this occurs because of values that ascribe low importance to children, and sometimes it happens primarily for financial reasons. Every additional mouth to feed is burdensome for Kenyans living in poverty, and as a result, many parents are unable to afford to meet the basic needs of all their children. When this is the case, sometimes parents will put one or more of their children in the care of a wealthier individual or family. Ideally, the kids end up living with a nearby relative, but sometimes the caretaker is a neighbor, another trusted community member, or an orphanage staffed by caring people.

Things were winding down at the school, so Dad, Raika, Kaitlyn, and I began gathering our belongings for the short trek to the orphanage. As we walked away, I looked over my shoulder one more time at Mosop School and smiled. I was happy to be there and looked forward to going back the next day.

There was no way for me to know, in that moment, what an indelible mark Mosop would leave on my life. God was going to use what happened at that school, with those kids, to begin weaving my story into the fabric of Africa. At Mosop he was going to start bringing clear purpose and direction to this lost, confused *mzungu*. He was going to help me see that in Kenya I could feel found instead of lost. He was going to show me that this unfamiliar country, with all its cultural differences and uncomfortable surprises, could be a place where my heart would feel at home.

# CHAPTER 6

# THE STUB OF A
## *Pencil*

*Er, er, er, er, ERRRRR!*

The neighborhood rooster was my alarm clock every morning at Mosop. When the rooster crowed, hitting "snooze" was not an option.

While we stayed at the orphanage, Raika, Kaitlyn, and I were roommates in the guest room. My dad had been relegated to a barn out back. We had two small twin beds and two mosquito nets to share among the three of us, so by the time I showed up, the other girls had already pushed the beds together and combined the mosquito nets in anticipation of my arrival. They offered me the middle of the bed, and I took it.

Mosop Orphanage was a large home as Kenyan houses go. Along with the guest room and the small barn, it had a kitchen, a living room, a master bedroom, and separate wings for the boys and girls who were living there. Still, although there were lots of rooms, the square footage per room was modest. In the guest room, when our bags were lined up along the walls, we had just enough space to walk around the edges of the bed.

When the rooster signaled sunrise, the three of us would untangle ourselves from our mosquito nets, climb out of bed, and start our morning. The first item on my agenda every day was putting off using the bathroom. My reasoning was straightforward: the toilet consisted of a hole in the ground. It wasn't outside, at least, but it was still a squatty potty, and it smelled. As much as I wanted to embrace differences in African culture, that one was a sticking point for me. I really, really preferred flushing toilets you could sit on.

Next came breakfast, which consisted of buttered bread and warm chai. It took skill to ask for the correct amount of bread. Unfortunately, I had a talent for requesting multiple pieces of bread only when it was stale. Whenever I declined a full stack and took only one piece, that piece would arrive on my plate perfectly fresh.

After breakfast, time in the classroom was punctuated by quarter-mile walks between the school and orphanage where we would eat lunch and take tea breaks. Dinner was always some kind of goat stew. Then we would stay up late talking with the headmaster, with music videos playing in the background. The orphanage had one VHS tape of Kenyan music videos, and every night the headmaster played that tape on a loop.

Even though we were at Mosop for less than a week, our pattern was so routine that my recollection of it is still vivid. If I needed to, I could probably go back today and pick up the sequence right where we left off. Still, there was one sliver of time, about forty minutes, that stood out from all the others.

My dad and I had volunteered in a classroom of first- and second-grade students. The room was fairly small, and aside from the exuberance of twenty or so kids, it was plain. Furnishings included a chalkboard, a desk for the teacher, and two low tables surrounded by kid-sized chairs. Unlike most of the elementary schoolrooms I had spent time in, there were no brightly colored *ABC* signs or *123* paper banners tacked onto the walls. Instead, this one featured a couple of old rice sacks: the teacher had converted them into educational posters by drawing little lessons on them with a marker and then hanging them up. In this learning environment, you just made do with what you had.

The kids were making do too. Since there weren't any desks, drawers, or cubbies for stowing their things, and since many of them didn't have backpacks either, most of their supplies were strewn across the two tables. The grand total still wasn't much—a few shabby sweaters, some screw-top canisters carrying what I assumed was lunch, and notebooks.

At first glance, the notebooks looked like scribble pads to me. They were about five inches by seven inches, and maybe an inch thick, with sometimes nearly every part of every page covered with writing. But as I looked closer, and as I watched how the class worked, I realized that the notebooks were the kids' lesson books. The teacher would write something on the chalkboard, then the students would practice writing the same thing in their books. When they did, they maximized every blank spot of paper they had.

"Children," the teacher announced, "today we will keep learning English words. Mr. Lucas and Miss Riley will be helping us."

Then she turned and wrote "ball" on the chalkboard, saying the letters as she wrote them. "B-a-l-l. Ball."

"Ball," the kids repeated.

One of the boys at my table carefully formed each letter, and when he struggled, I placed my hand gently on top of his to help him along. It took a little while for him to get his coordination down, and his pencil wasn't helping the situation because it had been ground down to a stub. Eventually, though, he got it.

"Great job!" I told him, clapping and giving his shoulders a squeeze. He smiled and giggled shyly.

When he was finished, I expected him to find another blank space in his notebook and practice *b-a-l-l* again. That's how I had learned to write letters: repetition on lined pieces of paper. Write the same letter over and over, and eventually you'll get it.

Instead, that young student took his stub of a pencil and passed it to the child next to him.

I had to look twice to make sure that what I was seeing was real. Around that little school table, with probably ten kids trying to learn their English alphabet, there was only a single writing utensil. All of them were sharing just that stub of a pencil!

By that point in our visit to Africa, I had recognized that schooling would greatly increase the Kenyan kids' chances of climbing out of poverty. Getting educated was their best bet. I also knew it was a big deal just to be enrolled in school; it meant that either you had a sponsor or your family had come up with enough money to buy a uniform and pay tuition fees. But what good was it to be on a class roster if you didn't have the basic tools for learning?

I stood up and walked over to the teacher.

"Do you have any more pencils?" I asked.

She shook her head.

"Pens?"

Again she answered, "No."

I peered over at my dad's table, only to realize that he was stuck in a similar conundrum: his kids were playing Pass the Pen.

Feeling around in the pockets of my skirt, I tried to find something that would be useful for writing. I looked for something on the floor too, but I came up empty. For the rest of the time in class, I followed the pencil around the table, helping whichever child was taking a turn with it. "Ball" took nearly twenty minutes, and the next word did too. Each student spent 90 percent of the class time waiting.

While it was great that they were all so good at sharing, I couldn't help but get frustrated, watching them take turns like that. Not only was it sad, but it also made me feel a bit foolish. I had brought a suitcase full of toys to Kenya, thinking that kids in poverty would find joy in playthings. In my rich, privileged life in the United States, it never would have occurred to me that a pencil could be a source of fulfillment and deep satisfaction. In my world, a pencil is just a pencil. I could have brought packs and packs of them to these kids!

⁕ ⁕ ⁕

Dad and I finished up our time in that classroom, and a couple of days later we finished up at the school and flew home. Between the two of us, we must have taken hundreds of Kenya stories back to Missouri. Of all of them, though, the classroom story—one pen and one stubby pencil for all those kids—was the one that struck me the most. I knew that without a good education, my young friends had an extremely limited future.

When we arrived home, the person who fielded most of my thoughts and stories about Kenya was my mom. For as long as I can remember, we've had a close bond, and whenever I've had something pressing on my heart—whether sorrow, confusion, joy, or triumph—I've wanted to share it with Mom. She also has a knack for helping steer me; when I'm stuck in my own intensity and emotion, my mom can usually chart a course for me that will work. As I was reflecting on my first trip to Africa, that skill came in handy, probably more than ever.

Mom and I were in the car one day, running some errands around town, and I was feeling sad, thinking of my Kenyan friends and missing them.

"I just want to go back," I told her. "Do you think I could go back?"

In hindsight, the request was pretty selfish and shortsighted, but my mom didn't say so. She also didn't point out that international flights are an expensive way to keep in touch. And she didn't hint that overseas travel isn't something that teenagers should attempt on a whim. Instead, she thought for a minute.

"You can't go back just to go back," she told me. "You'd have to go back and *do* something."

"What do you think I could do?"

"Well, you keep talking about the little kids trying to write with no pencils. I can tell that's hard for you to think about."

Then in her matter-of-fact, straight-to-the-point way, she made a simple suggestion. It was an idea that would reverberate in our lives, in our family's and friends', in our hometown, and in Kenya for years to come: "Maybe you could go back and do something about *that*."

CHAPTER 7

# GENERATION *Next*

Motivated by my mom's challenge, we decided as a family that Mom was going to be joining Dad and me on our second trip to Kenya. Our whole family was excited about this for lots of reasons, including a key logistical one: having a third person on the trip was going to increase our luggage allowance by three bags. We would be able to take a lot more with us to help the African children.

We thought we knew how we would get donations for our trip. We thought it was going to be no trouble at all. Our plan was simple: we would visit all the big superstores around town and some office supply stores too. We would find a manager, ask for a contribution, and easily get one. Because who could resist helping needy kids?

As it turned out, a lot of people could, and did.

As I've learned over the years, there is no telling which doors God will open or how he'll do it. In the same way, there is no way to predict which ones will stay closed or why. Whenever I think I have his plan figured out, it's almost inevitable that he's going to surprise me.

The first time Mom and I went to a store to make a big request, the interaction went like this: We asked to see a manager and then waited for the manager. When he arrived, I gave him my best thirty-second description of our upcoming trip, including why we needed what we needed. I finished with a big smile and what felt like an irresistible proposal: "We know your store carries a lot of great school supplies, and we're here today hoping you'll be willing to contribute some for these Kenyan kids who need so much. Would you be willing to do that?"

The manager nodded encouragingly. It seemed like he was sold.

"Okay, yeah—that sounds great. Sounds like a great cause. Just come with me, and I'll get you the form to fill out."

He did a half turn and started leading us down the aisle toward the back of the store. We walked excitedly alongside him.

"Thanks so much!" we told him. "We really appreciate it."

"No problem. Pleasure."

He kept walking, then almost offhandedly, he said, "You'll need your tax-exempt number. Do you have that with you?"

Our tax-exempt number. Why would we have a tax-exempt number?

"Sorry?" I told him. "We don't have a tax-exempt number."

He slowed and then brought us all to a stop.

"Oh. Okay. Sorry, but if you want to apply for a donation, you have to have tax-exempt status. You don't have a nonprofit? Like a 501(c)3?"

"I'm not—" I stammered, shaking my head. "I don't have any of that."

His shoulders dropped, and I could see he felt a little defeated for us.

"Sorry, the only kind of donating we do is to tax-exempt organizations. That way we can write off what we give you."

My mom and I let his words and the disappointment sink in.

"So, because we're not a nonprofit, we can't even apply for a donation?" my mom asked.

He shook his head. "Sorry, I wish I could help you."

She sighed. I sighed. We thanked him for his time and for his kind explanation, and we left. At the next store, we talked with a different manager but had a practically identical conversation. And then we did it again at the next store after that, and at the next one after that. It took just a few hours for us to see that that rejection pattern was bound to keep repeating itself all across town.

Soon after that, though, my mom ran into a family friend. He knew we were heading back to Kenya the following summer, so he asked about how our trip plans were going. Mom explained that some of them were going well, but we were having a hard time getting donations of supplies because we weren't set up as a tax-exempt entity.

"Rough. Yeah, that's a pretty standard practice these days."

Suddenly it occurred to my mom that our family friend was an accountant.

"Hey—do you have any experience with setting up nonprofits?"

"Lots, actually."

"You do? What's the process like?"

"It's pretty quick after you get through the pile of paperwork."

"Really?"

"Really. In fact, it's something I do fairly often. So how about this: if you guys decide to file, just let me know, and I'll be happy to do the paperwork for you."

Not long after that, with our friend's generous help, we began the process of filing for nonprofit status. We chose a name for our organization: Generation Next. The idea was that if we could help educate one generation of kids in Kenya, then those kids would be able to pour income and marketable skills back into their villages and hometowns, benefiting the generation to come. The way we saw it, the more children we could help educate, the higher the chances that families and communities would be lifted out of poverty in the future.

The paperwork was completed and approved, turning me into the head of a nonprofit organization at age fourteen. I was excited about having a way to get my hands on more school supplies for Kenya. In my mind, that was the extent of Generation Next: just a one-girl operation—me, with my family behind me, getting donations for African kids in need. None of us expected that it would evolve into anything more.

Once again, that was what we thought we knew. But God was about to give us a few crash courses in *his* vision for Generation Next—and that involved throwing us for some big loops.

# CHAPTER 8

# OPERATION
## *Teenager*

Right from the start, things didn't happen the way we had hoped they would. With my freshly minted nonprofit papers in hand, I sat at our kitchen table and tried to restart the donation-collection process. I called up several different local store managers and introduced myself as the founder of Generation Next. Then, after telling them about the project we were working on for Kenya, I highlighted a few of the items we needed most and asked if they would be willing to contribute.

A few of them said they could donate some things. That part was wonderful. On more than one occasion, however, I got the sense that some of the nondonating managers weren't taking me seriously.

"It's because I'm so young, isn't it?" I asked my mom. She was sitting with me while I made the calls, offering support.

"Hopefully not," she said. "I don't know. Maybe."

We both slumped forward a little at the thought. Then we sat there quietly for a few minutes, frowning slightly and resting our elbows on the table. I propped my chin on one of my palms. My mom drummed her fingers. Then she shrugged.

"Why don't I give it a try," she said, reaching for the phone.

Mom called up one of the managers whom I felt might have blown me off. She introduced herself as being affiliated with Generation Next, and then just as I had done, she quickly described our project, gave a short list of needs, and asked for a donation. Her phrasing was slightly different from mine in a few places, but overall it was pretty close to a duplicate of the pitch I had made. When she hung up the phone, she had a promised donation in the bag.

I wish I could tell you it was the only time that sort of thing happened, but it wasn't. On many more occasions, my mom has called up a person who just finished denying my request, only to have them respond favorably to hers. With nearly identical talking points, she would get a yes while I got a no.

Many times I was insecure about being a teenage leader, even as the head of a nonprofit as tiny as Generation Next was at the time. I was worried that people wouldn't take our work seriously because of me. I was anxious about how to handle the organization's finances. I feared that sometime down the road, in a moment of fiery teenage emotion or apathy, I might lose interest in Kenya and scrap the whole thing. I agonized about leaving people in the lurch as a result.

So when adults seemed to raise their eyebrows skeptically, and when managers seemed to discriminate based solely on the maturity of my vocal chords, it felt like a confirmation of all the doubts I was trying to push down. It implied that the principle hurdle to our funding and support wasn't the fact that we were a small, locally run operation; the obstacle was *me*.

I was baffled about what to do with that. There was no way to age myself any faster, and I couldn't suddenly improve the whole world's perception of teenagers. At times the only sensible option seemed to be giving control to someone else, someone older and more experienced. It seemed like our prospects would be better that way, so on several occasions I toyed with the idea. Certainly my mom or dad could handle the role. They were trustworthy, they were both doing a lot of work for Generation Next already, and they were adults, so other adults would probably respond more favorably to them.

Still, I never asked them to consider leading Generation Next, and they wouldn't have accepted the role if I had. We had been aware all along that a teenage leader for Generation Next wasn't the standard, conventional way of doing things. None of us was surprised to find that our decision came with a particular set of pitfalls. From the beginning, we had suspected it would—and we had made the choice anyway. I suppose if any of us had been interested in making Generation Next a "success" by worldly standards, our criteria for selecting a leader would have been different. We would have sought someone who wears a suit Monday through Friday, someone who could comfortably rub elbows with big-time donors. Business savvy and fund-raising experience would have been deal breakers. But an eighth-grader? Must be some kind of joke.

Nevertheless, our original reasons for putting me in charge didn't change. We all felt that God had put a rush of love for Kenyan children in my heart, and he had put an impulse in me that made me want to figure out some ways to help them. That was why Generation Next had come to be. It was why we were busy making phone calls for school supplies in the first place. So we carried on, once again asking God to give us all we would need to be faithful and see things through. We needed him to give us strength and tenacity to stay the course and to trust that when he put a teenager at the center of this thing, he knew exactly what he was doing.

Which, of course, he absolutely did. It didn't take long before that was plainer than anything.

# CHAPTER 9

# LITTLE KIDS
## *Giving Big*

When you spend most of your spare time trying to gather up educational supplies for kids, sooner or later you start thinking about elementary schools.

As my family and I worked to collect items for young students in Kenya, it occurred to us that most American kids start each school year with far more supplies than they'll actually use. Particularly in the youngest grades, kids are so loaded up with pencils, erasers, and crayons in September that they still have stockpiles in June.

In Branson alone there were four elementary schools, and every single student in those schools had started the year with a full list of recommended supplies. It was almost as if they were asking Generation Next to start up a collection. More to the point, though, elementary school kids seemed to fit in perfectly with what our organization was working to do. Who better than kids to support a ministry for kids that was run by a kid? Who better than one slightly older kid to be the catalyst for mobilizing several hundred other kids to give?

My brother Cameron had a friend on his basketball team whose parents worked for the Branson school district, and because our two families were always cheering for the boys at their games, we had gotten to know each other pretty well. We told them we had a school supplies drive in mind for Kenya and asked what it would take to get the idea approved. They responded by volunteering to ask the principals in the district if it would be okay. We got the green light quickly and easily, and before we knew it, Generation Next was raising donations.

Needing a way to collect supplies in each of the four schools, we got our hands on some extra-large, heavy-duty cardboard boxes. We made several signs that said, "Drop your school supplies here!" under a Generation Next logo, and we printed up an informational flyer for every teacher. We put a sign and a couple of boxes in the main hallway at each school, and we distributed all the flyers. Then we waited to see what would happen.

It was mid-April when the drive started, just before spring break and two months before summer vacation, but it didn't take long before the boxes started filling up. Both of my brothers were elementary age that year, so our family could easily track the progress of the collection at their school, whether by having the boys check the boxes or by stopping in at drop-off or pickup time. Each of the other schools was kind enough to give us a call every time their boxes were getting full, and then we would do a round of supply pickups.

Excitement about Kenya was clearly catching on. Kids were tossing all kinds of school goodies into our collection boxes. Some teachers, we learned, had cleaned out their supply closets to give as much as possible to Generation Next. At one of the schools, we were even getting some extra advertising: someone, probably a staff member, had hung up a big map of Africa with a star over Kenya, to show kids and parents where the donations would be going.

By the time the last week of school arrived, it had become clear that unless something changed in our family's living arrangements, we weren't going to have enough room at home for all the donated supplies. For a while we had been stowing our loot at several locations all around the house, but that random piling system was getting out of hand.

So one day when it came time to do a round of pickups, my parents backed both the family vehicles out of our garage, and we gave the floor a good sweeping. Then we drove off and rounded up four giant stashes of donated school supplies. When we got them home with us, both cars stayed outside, and the first-ever Generation Next command center rolled in. When we had our entire haul sorted, we had bag after bag of pencils and box after box of mostly new crayons. There were markers, colored pencils, scissors, erasers, blank notebooks, and unopened packages of paper—and these were just the end-of-school-year leftovers from just *some* of the kids in our school district. It was an astounding reminder of the excess that so many Western households live with all the time.

"You know," my dad remarked as we sifted through supplies, "in most families around here, this stuff would have gone home on the last day of school and gotten stuffed in a drawer for the summer. By the time fall came around again, nobody would remember it was there, and they would go out and buy all new supplies again for the school year."

He was right; that was what our family had always done, and most of our friends did it too. We all had a drawer somewhere full of random pencils and pens—a perfectly good stash of writing utensils. But when the calendar turned to September each year and the school supplies lists went out, none of us thought to fulfill the list with our gently used supplies. Instead, we usually bought new. Some years we even discarded and replaced perfectly good backpacks, and judging by the contents of the boxes we had picked up, a lot of other local kids did too.

All together we had collected just over two hundred kids'

backpacks and plenty of school supplies to fill them. Some of the items were new donations from friends of ours and stores we had reached out to, but most of the stash had been given by elementary school kids. What an incredibly beautiful picture: kids helping kids, kids learning about other kids' needs and then reaching out to meet them. It fit our mission in ways that were bigger and better than we had ever intended.

When we had named Generation Next, we had had one "next" generation in mind, and it was a geographical one: kids in Kenya. Our organization was about helping and serving them so they could help and serve in their own communities, especially a few years down the road. But now we were working with a "next" on our side of the ocean as well: helping to mobilize kids in the local region to rally behind the cause.

And to our surprise, a couple of them were looking to rally in an especially meaningful, personal way.

CHAPTER 10

# *Kid*

# MISSIONARIES

Shortly after I returned from my first trip to Kenya, my friend Hadley and I organized an event in Branson to raise awareness about another East African country. We had learned that a brutal regime was wreaking havoc in northern Uganda. Among other atrocities, it was violently displacing families from their homes and communities. One of the worst parts of the tragedy was that most people in the world had no idea it was going on. The victims were predominantly poor and vulnerable, and they had little representation on the world's stage.

Hadley and I cringed at the injustice of it. We felt those displaced persons deserved a voice just like everybody does, so we wanted to do something to help get the word out. Like many young people who were beginning to advocate for this tragedy at the time, Hadley and I planned an overnight event to help ourselves and others get a small taste of what it's like to be displaced. We got some necessary approvals, including speaking with a school official and convincing our parents to supervise, and then we invited our classmates to spend a whole night on a field at our local elementary school. The premise was simple and cheap: each person would bring a cardboard box, and we would all use our boxes to make individual shelters to sleep in. We had a decent turnout, with many of our classmates and even a few additional parents participating. None of us was thrilled at the prospect of sleeping in a box hut, and we talked a lot about what it might feel like to actually have to do so.

As daylight faded, Hadley and I had a long conversation about my time in Kenya. I didn't yet know for sure whether I'd be going back, so I talked mostly about what I'd seen. On that night, of all nights, with our focus on the needs of vulnerable East Africans, it felt fitting to reflect on the poverty I'd witnessed in Kenya. I told Hadley about the bin babies, about the kids playing outside in the streets, and about the classroom of students sharing their pen and pencil. I told her how terrible it had felt, having only toys to give them instead of something more useful. I told her how badly I wanted to go back.

A few months later, when I found out that I was returning to Kenya for sure, I remembered that night on the school field and how Hadley and I had connected over memories and dreams of East Africa. I made a point to find her at school and tell her I was going back.

"You are?" She clapped her hands together excitedly. "I'm so excited for you!"

"Thanks, I'm really excited too."

We talked for a while about what my parents and I were planning to do, and both of us got more and more animated. Finally, it was just too much emotion for Hadley to keep in check.

"Aw," she exclaimed, "I wish I could go along!"

"Oh, that would be so cool, wouldn't it?"

"Really cool," she said, nodding.

A slight frown was forming at the corners of her mouth. We both looked off down the hallway for a moment, feeling bad. Then suddenly I had an idea.

"Hey, maybe I could ask my parents if you could come with us, if you want me to."

Hadley's jaw dropped.

"Really? You think you could do that?"

"Sure. I mean, I don't know if they'll say yes, but it won't hurt to ask."

She jumped up and down and gave me a quick squeeze. "That would be so great! Oh, now I really, really want to go!"

That evening at home, I brought up the possibility to my parents. Hadley was a longtime friend of mine, and our two families had been close for years as well, so if anybody had a shot at coming with us, it was somebody like her. Still, I knew it was a potentially thorny idea, asking my mom and dad to consider chaperoning her. She was somebody else's young teen daughter, and our trip was going to entail all kinds of potential risks: international travel, African wildlife, and nearly two weeks serving out in the Kenyan bush. Adding another minor to the trip would be putting a lot on their shoulders.

When I initially asked my mom, though, her response was about as positive as Hadley or I could have hoped for. She didn't freak out, and she told me that she and my dad would think it over. This nonrejection elated me. It meant there was a chance!

My parents took some time to pray about it and talk things through. They weighed the potential dangers and discussed how a fourth person would impact our trip's logistics. There were plenty of things to be cautious about, and they knew that—still, they didn't see any glaring red flags. So we talked with Hadley's family in detail about international travel, volunteering in Kenya, the necessary fees and expenses, and what it would all entail. In the end, each of us felt comfortable with the idea of Hadley making the trip, and all four parents gave it a green light.

It's possible that there have never been two people more excited than Hadley and I were after that! Whenever we were together, it was like someone had turned up a couple of dials on our voices; all our giddy words tumbled out high-pitched and rapid-fire. We spent hours discussing what each of us was going to pack. We buried our noses in online satellite images of Kenya and photos from my first trip. We were enthusiastic about fund-raising and asking more businesses for donations. We couldn't wait to book plane tickets and confirm our departure date, because then we could start a Kenya countdown. We were even looking forward to getting our travel shots. We had more than enough enthusiasm for the two of us, so it shouldn't have come as a surprise when we found out that excitement for our trip had spread.

Hadley and I had another friend, Gio, who was our classmate and whose family belonged to the same church as my family. Gio and his mom and dad all knew about Generation Next and what we were doing in Kenya. They thought it was wonderful that we were experiencing a new culture together and serving within it. So when they got wind of the fact that we had expanded our second trip to include Hadley, they started wondering if additional openings might be available. Gio wanted to go too!

Before we knew it, we were all having detailed discussions again about travel and serving and funds, and our Kenya trip roster was expanding from four to five. In just a few short months, what had started out as a single-family service project had become a group effort with three different households represented. Generation Next, which we had intended to be just a vehicle for accepting donations, had not only completed a successful donation drive, but we were now about to host what was essentially an overseas mission trip for three kids instead of one. And we would be representing hundreds of Branson schoolchildren as well.

Our little team couldn't have been more excited. We had ten hands on deck instead of six, and we had fifteen suitcases instead of nine to be filled up with school stuff. The trip was going to be spectacular; we were all confident about it. The only problem was we still hadn't figured out exactly where the five of us and all our bags would be going in Kenya or how we would get there.

CHAPTER 11

# Muma

We thought we were headed back to Bomet. The only people we had ever worked with in Kenya were there, so that was a decision that practically made itself. We were expecting to serve at both Tenwek and Mosop again, and we were looking to volunteer at a few additional schools as well; that way we could be sure to pass out all the supplies we were bringing along. Our challenge was to identify some reliable, trustworthy partners who could help cart us around, host us, and arrange to get our work done in the country. We knew it amounted to a lot, but on our first trip Dad and I had established a number of good friendships with missionaries and aid workers, and most of them were well connected locally. We had every reason to believe that with their help we would get everything sorted out. And for a while that's exactly what seemed to be happening.

The headmaster and his wife at Mosop School and Orphanage were happy to make room for us again, and they were thrilled we wanted to visit their school. Since we were expecting to pay for transportation, they told us that getting to and from their area would be no problem. After only a few emails back and forth with them, we knew we would be all set for the Mosop leg of our trip. But serving at Mosop wouldn't be enough to keep us all busy for two and a half weeks, and unfortunately, none of the other sites were coming together nearly as well.

For some reason, no matter how hard we tried, and no matter how hard our Kenyan friends tried, we could not find a place to stay in Bomet. This was incredibly frustrating, because Dad and I knew that the missionaries there were kind and generous. And having stayed in the row of doctors' apartments before, we also knew that there was plenty of room to fit five extra people for a few days. Everything seemed bound to add up in our favor—we were sure of it.

We reached out to all the friends Dad and I had made from our first year, and Uncle Logan and Aunt Julie, who had returned to the States, contacted some of their friends for us too. Everyone we spoke with was eager to help, but each one of them also had some fluke that prevented them from hosting us. Many were leaving Kenya before we would arrive. Some were going to be traveling when we expected to be coming through. Some already knew they would have other guests visiting. Each person who had to say no to us was happy to introduce us to someone else who might be able to help, but even when we traced those referrals, we kept arriving at dead ends.

Weeks and weeks passed, turning into months and months. We all believed that God had brought our group together because he wanted us in Kenya, and we all believed that he already had our trip figured out down to the minute already. There was no need to be anxious about the gaping holes in our plan, right? Still, the uncertainty was starting to feel stressful.

Then, one day at school, my friend Ali approached me. She knew I was going to Kenya, and she wanted to tell me about her aunt, who was sponsoring a teenager there. His name was Mumo, and Ali said that she'd told him about me. He was interested in friending me on Facebook because he'd heard about my heart for Kenyan kids.

"Okay, yeah," I told her. "It would probably be cool to talk with him a little."

If I'd had an inkling of what God was in the process of doing, it might have been difficult for me to handle the thrill! The beauty of watching God work is that his ways are so utterly unlike ours that often his moves seem to come out of nowhere. In the middle of doing what you think you should do, with prayer and faith underlying it all, still there are times when he's up to something totally different.

A few days after Ali and I talked, Mumo's friend request appeared in my Facebook feed. On his profile he indicated that he lived in Kibwezi. I typed it into my search engine and learned that Kibwezi is located on the eastern side of Kenya, between Nairobi and the Indian Ocean. My friends in Bomet were on the other side of the country's capital, toward the center of the continent. It was a good six-and-a-half-hour drive from Mumo to anyone else I knew in Africa.

Mumo and I got to know each other a little at a time. We would ask a few questions and share a few details, and then Mumo would remind me that Generation Next was always welcome to come visit him in Kibwezi, where my friend's aunt's sponsorship enabled him to go to school. In my mind, it made no sense to drive all that way in the opposite direction of where we planned to serve. We couldn't go east because we already knew we were going west; we were just waiting for our contacts in Bomet to come through. But Mumo and I kept talking, and he told me about Namba, the charitable organization that managed his sponsorship. We got to know each other pretty well, and it was good to have him as a friend, even without the option of an East Kenya meet-up.

But then, before I knew it, four months had passed since my first online chat with Mumo. It was just two months out from our scheduled trip. Our team had been knocking on every Kenyan door, and still we didn't have all our basic resources lined up in Bomet. The five of us had begun to think that maybe we needed to try a different angle. Were we supposed to go to Kibwezi? Could we?

My parents and I had already done a little research about Namba and its charity work, so we knew it operated exclusively in Kibwezi and was doing good things there. Namba was in the process of constructing a building in hopes that it could be converted into an orphanage. The charity was also managing a long-term school sponsorship program (Mumo was one of the recipients), hosting medical clinics, and pursuing some sustainable farming initiatives locally. Its founder, Robin, lived in the United States ten months out of the year and traveled to Kibwezi the remaining two months to oversee Namba's projects in person.

My parents and I started sending messages back and forth with Robin, telling her about our work and our recent connection with Mumo, and it wasn't long before we connected with her by phone. We talked with her about our desire to help school-aged kids in Kenya and asked if there might be opportunities for us to do that in Kibwezi.

"Oh sure. There are plenty. My contacts through Namba could set you up with lots of schools to visit."

"Wow, that would be great."

"And there's a little guesthouse in town where your group could stay. We could easily arrange a ride for you to and from the Nairobi airport, plus transportation while you're local."

"Wow. We, uh—thank you! Maybe that could work."

We told Robin we would get back to her soon. When we hung up, the three of us sat there dumbfounded, amazed at what had just happened. Up until then, we had been so baffled about why God seemed to be closing the door on Bomet. We were convinced that he had work for us in Kenya, and we thought that Bomet was our only option. But then God opened a door in Kibwezi, powerfully and obviously.

We did a little more research. We contacted our friends at Tenwek and Mosop to apologize and say we'd had an unexpected change of plans. Then our group booked five round-trip flights to Nairobi, and I wrote one especially exciting message to my new friend in Kibwezi.

"Guess what, Mumo? We're coming to see you."

# CHAPTER 12

# From West
## to East

G etting to Kibwezi was a two-day journey. As far as travel to
Kenya goes, that's pretty typical. There isn't a major airport
in Branson, so no matter where we catch our initial departing
flight, the first leg of our route is an hour-long road trip. From
there it takes one or two flights (or more) to get ourselves across
the Atlantic, generally into Amsterdam. After that we have at least
one more flight before reaching Nairobi, where our first step is
immigration and customs.

With a whole team of people and all the gear we bring, the
port-of-entry process takes a while even in a best-case scenario.
Kenyan airport officials aren't above requesting payment to help
keep things moving—call it a bribe and you'd be right—so the
process doesn't naturally lend itself to speed. By the time we clear
customs, we've generally spent almost twenty hours in the air and
ten to twenty more in airport terminals. We're eight hours ahead
of our bodies' internal clocks, and nobody can figure out what
time of day or night it is. All that and we still have a four-hour
drive ahead of us to our destination. It's a haul no matter how you
slice it.

When we arrived at Nairobi International for the second time, we had been eating airport food, snoozing on airport furniture and floors, and lugging our carry-on bags around for more than forty hours. Our bodies were craving exercise and decent sleep. We'd had emotional good-byes with our families at the start of the trip, and we hadn't been able to get through Kenyan immigration without handing over ten of the Bibles we had brought with us. But then suddenly our passports were all stamped and approved, and we were about to exit the terminal together, and it was wonderful.

"Riley! Lucas! Tracy!"

Spotting Mumo was easy. He was jumping, waving, shouting, and giggling on the lower level of the airport as we made our way down from above. I recognized him instantly. Still, I almost did a double take at the sight and sound of him. If I hadn't known he was in his early twenties, I might have put him at twelve or thirteen. The man he was standing with towered over him.

*That must be Burgwin*, I thought.

We had initially learned about Burgwin through Robin, during our earliest talks with her. We had been discussing what we hoped to accomplish in Kenya, all of us knowing that Robin wasn't due to be in Kibwezi while we were there. Since she would still be in the States, she had wanted to make sure we had a good local contact, specifically someone who would help take care of us and get us where we needed to go. When she heard we were looking to help out young students, she had recommended Burgwin to us right away. And when she listed off some of his character traits and skills, we guessed he'd be a great fit.

By training, Burgwin is a social worker. It's his job to travel in and around Kibwezi, working with kids at various schools in the region, so he's well connected with lots of local educators. He also knows English well enough to translate it. Robin had felt comfortable suggesting him to us because he'd often helped out with Namba projects; she could personally vouch for his work ethic and reliability.

Burgwin had cleared his schedule so he could come along with us most days to translate. He had also booked our rooms in Kibwezi and made arrangements with all the schools we were going to visit. He had even coordinated with one Kibwezi school for us to host their students at a three-day vacation Bible school. Short of booking our flights and collecting school supplies back in the United States, we could credit Burgwin and Mumo with taking care of pretty much everything we expected to need for our visit.

We had asked Mumo to take a break from school and come stay with us for the duration of our trip, and he had agreed. That put our head count for the ride to Kibwezi at eight, including our driver, and we also had nine or ten carry-ons and large suitcases. Wisely, Burgwin had hired a driver who came with a van, but even in the jumbo vehicle we had to tie a bunch of our bags to the roof.

Our route out of Nairobi was on a single stretch of pavement, Mombasa Road, named after the port city Mombasa, which sits on Kenya's Indian Ocean coastline. The year before, my dad and I had traveled in the opposite direction out of Nairobi: northwest, toward Lake Victoria and the lush, green areas that surround it. Mombasa Road would take us into an entirely different sort of countryside—although in the dimness, there was no way for any of us to see that, and even if it had been visible, I'm not sure we would have been awake anyway.

It was nearly dark when we started out, and most of us slept most of the way. At one point Hadley and I were both awake and looking outside when our van's headlights lit the words on a road sign, informing us that Kibwezi was less than thirty kilometers away. When the reality set in that we would be there in fifteen minutes or less, it was impossible for us to keep that news to ourselves. I poked both of my parents. Hadley nudged Gio and Mumo. Everybody got really excited, and from then on, all sleeping in the van was pretty much over.

As we completed the last stretch, we all talked in animated voices about the work we would be doing soon. It was still too dark for us to see much of the area outside the van, so instead, we peppered Mumo and Burgwin with questions about it. A couple of us zipped open our backpacks to show them some of the toys and supplies we had brought to give away. Before we knew it, the car was slowing its pace and turning left off Mombasa Road.

Mumo leaned forward and pointed up ahead.

"This is Kibwezi," he said, and he smiled a proud, wide smile.

The village was small; it took only a couple of minutes and three turns before we reached our destination, which lay at the far edge of town. The van pulled to a stop in front of a tall iron gate. Our driver used the gate's intercom system to call inside the complex and announce our arrival. A few seconds later, the gate swung open, and we pulled into the parking area at Kambua Guest House, our Kibwezi home.

Kambua is about the size of a single-family home in the States. A sitting room at the center splits the building in half, with several rooms down each of two hallways on either side. The guest rooms are all identical, with one full-size bed, a small shelving unit that doubles as a nightstand, a desk, and a bathroom. If you want a couch or a great view, you go to one of the common areas. Aside from the central sitting room, there is a kitchen, a small conference and events area, and an outdoor terrace.

Kibwezi was the Africa that I had always pictured Africa to be. The land was flat and dry. Canopies on trees were low, sparse, and sprawling. The ground was a parched, rust-colored clay. Everything felt inexplicably right.

Over the course of our first Kambua meal—one egg each, a little fruit, and buttered white toast—we asked Mumo questions about Kibwezi, and he gave us the lay of the land and explained daily life in the town. Kibwezi was small, he said, but it had a

Hadley and I in the guest room

post office, a police station, and a couple of churches. He pointed one way and explained that it was east, toward the coast. Then he pointed about ninety degrees the other way.

"Over there is Kilimanjaro," he told us. "On a clear day, you can see it."

We *oohed* and *aahed*, and for a few minutes we all squinted out over the plain, trying to make out the shape of the mountain. The air was so hot and dry that the space just above the horizon turned into a fuzzy trick of light. I couldn't have known it at the time, but that view was a fitting metaphor for the two weeks that stretched out in front of us. In the midst of wonderful brightness, there is often disconcerting darkness. And yet above, around, and all through that hazy blur, a dawn is breaking.

# CHAPTER 13

# THE *BODA-BODA* *Business*

The next day, there was a lot of clapping and a lot of beaming, and a lot of nervous excitement filled the air. It was Saturday, our first full day in Kibwezi, and Burgwin had made arrangements for us to go to a nearby orphanage whose students were educated in-house. We couldn't wait to get there and spend time with the kids. After another one-egg breakfast at Kambua, Mumo and the five of us Americans gathered eagerly in the guesthouse sitting room, a pile of gear at our feet.

On the previous afternoon, we had stuffed our personal backpacks and a couple of duffel bags with kids' backpacks, and we had stuffed *those* backpacks with all kinds of things. Each kid at the orphanage would be getting a Bible, a notebook, some new pencils, a pencil sharpener, and one set of coloring tools, either markers or crayons, in his or her backpack. We were also bringing a few deflated soccer balls and some hand pumps for everybody at the orphanage to share. It was just a sliver of the load we had brought with us, but it was the start, and we were giddy about that. After months of legwork, the supplies people had donated were going to be placed in Kenyan kids' hands.

"What time is it?" I asked, looking around for a clock.

My dad checked his watch. "Ten twenty-three."

"Okay," I sighed, trying not to get too antsy.

Dad shrugged and flashed me a knowing smile. We had experienced this phenomenon the year before too: in Kenya "prompt" tends to be a fluid concept.

We waited a little while longer for our ride, taking some pictures and checking then rechecking our bags to keep busy. About thirty-five minutes after our coordinated pickup—not terrible, as Kenyan wait times go—in a roar of engine rumbles and mechanical spurts, Burgwin and our chariots arrived.

For the most part, taxis in Kenya have only two wheels. If you need to get somewhere and it's too far to walk, generally you hire a *boda-boda*, which is a simple, motorized dirt bike with a long seat attached over the rear wheel. The name *boda-boda* comes from one of their earliest uses (possibly their original use) in Kenya. Back in the day, along the border with Uganda, many travelers wanted to avoid walking the distance of the no-man's land between the two countries' checkpoints, but traditional taxis required lots of special paperwork and approvals to operate in the area. Some drivers showed up on the dirt bikes and started offering rides on the long seats. The bikes could work in no-man's land without requiring reams of extra paperwork, and because of their low fuel consumption, they could take people border to border (or, as it was pronounced, *boda-boda*) for a small fee.

Not surprisingly, the *boda-boda* business has taken off all over Kenya. Most of the region is well suited for it, especially in rural areas where most people don't need and/or can't afford a vehicle. If locals can hop on a motorbike taxi to get to their destination more quickly, then that's typically good enough. Most traveling Americans, if they're up for the cultural experience, will find that *boda-bodas* can take care of them pretty well too.

"Good morning!" Burgwin bounced into the guesthouse with a grin and a flourish. "The *boda-bodas* are here!"

After hugs and handshakes all around, he helped us grab our bags and haul them out to the front of the guesthouse where our rides were idling on the pavement. Burgwin helped translate as we introduced ourselves to the three drivers. Since Burgwin had ridden in on the backseat of one *boda-boda*, and since he was going to be coming with us to translate, that left two full seats and a partial for the six of us from Kambua. The passenger seats were clearly meant to fit more than one person, but it looked like putting three on any one of them was going to be a tight squeeze. In the end we decided that my mom and dad would ride together on one *boda-boda*, Gio would ride with Burgwin on another, and Mumo, Hadley, and I would round it out together on the third. When Burgwin saw that everyone was settled in, he patted the arm of his driver and waved a go-ahead to both of the others. One by one, they flicked their wrists back to rev their engines and switch into gear, and we were off.

HADLEY AND I ON THE BODA-BODA WITH OUR DRIVER

That was how nearly every morning in Kibwezi began. We rumbled away down a dry, red road, with multiple bags of goodies on our backs and several destinations plotted on our schedule. We wouldn't return to the guesthouse until late in the afternoon or sometimes the early evening, after visiting schools, inquiring about needs, passing out supplies, and spending time with the children. Our *boda-boda* drivers would deposit the whole Generation Next group back at Kambua, then take off for more work elsewhere.

Except on one day, when Hadley, Gio, Mumo, and I took a shortcut to the market alone. Our group had just returned from a full day out at schools. It was a hot and dry afternoon like Kenyan afternoons always seem to be. After dropping off our bags in our guest rooms, my dad lay down to take a nap, my mom grabbed a seat on the terrace with her journal and a pen, and Hadley, Gio, Mumo, and I were feeling hungry and thirsty as usual. We had been hoping to fill our stomachs that night by cooking our own dinner at the guesthouse. To do that safely, we knew we needed to get to the village, shop the market, and make it back to Kambua before dusk.

Around and through the center of town there are only three roads. If you look at the town on a map, the shape of two of the roads together is a lumpy, backward capital D. Kambua is located just above the top curve of the D. To get to the market from there by road, you follow the curve, the lump, and the curve again, until you run into the market street, Kibwezi's third road.

By contrast, the shortcut is a footpath, and it's about as direct a route as you'll get. Starting at Kambua, it's nearly a straight shot to the market's vendors. The problem with this shortcut is that it first winds through some patches of empty land on the north side of town, and then it turns into alleyways, which weave themselves among tight clusters of Kibwezi's tin homes and buildings. The shorter distance is great, but when you're the group of new white kids in town, alleyways and patches of empty land aren't necessarily the safest places to be.

For the first week and a half of our time in Kibwezi, whenever we walked to the market, Hadley, Gio, Mumo, and I always took at least one adult with us on the shortcut. If ever we were by ourselves, we had kept to the roads. Then came the night when we wanted to cook but had limited time before dusk to buy our ingredients. I asked my mom if we could take the shortcut without her.

"Are you sure you *need* to take the shortcut?"

"It's 5:20 already, Mom. I think the sun set around 6:30 last night."

"Okay," she said, "you guys can go, as long as Mumo stays with you. Deal?"

"Deal!"

The four of us bolted toward the door. We walked down the guesthouse drive toward Kambua's gate, gabbing about what we were going to shop for. As the gate opened to let us exit, we saw the three *boda-bodas* we had been riding all day, idling at the side of the road. We smiled and waved at the drivers, and they smiled back. Then we found the footpath we needed and kept walking.

Our little group wasn't far down the path when we heard rumbles and clicks coming up behind us. We turned around and saw the three *boda-boda* drivers. As they approached us, we all moved to the side of the path so they could pass, but none of them took that hint. Instead, they matched our speed, following just behind us. One of them said something in Swahili, and Mumo stopped and turned back toward them so he could answer.

Hadley, Gio, and I were used to tuning out conversations in Swahili by then, and we were still in a hurry to get our groceries, so we kept walking, expecting Mumo's conversation to be finished right away. But after we had continued on for a minute or so and he still hadn't caught up with us, we turned around and went back to find him.

Mumo was standing in front of the three *boda-boda* drivers, motioning earnestly with his hands. They had been accommodating to us all day, but now they looked cocky. The one at the front of the group was leaning forward onto his bike's blue handgrips, glaring. When Hadley, Gio, and I walked up to the group, the conversation stalled, and Blue Grips gestured toward me with a nod.

"You did not pay us enough money," he told me, gesturing toward his friends and then himself. He leaned back on the seat of his *boda-boda* and crossed his arms over his chest.

Right away I had an idea of where the conversation was headed, and it made me furious. I knew we had paid them good money already—I had even watched the transaction take place. Now these three grown men were trying to intimidate a group of teenagers into giving them more. My blood was boiling.

"First of all, *I* didn't pay you," I said. "My *dad* did. And if you need more, you can go back to where *he* is—where you just came from."

I—me, shy me—looked them directly in the eyes as I spat out the words. My pulse was racing and my nerves were tingling, but this was wrong, and I wasn't about to let them get away with it.

Blue's arms were still crossed, and he had barely registered my indignation. "You did not pay me enough," he repeated.

I narrowed my eyes at him, intent on countering his intimidation. "We'll just go," I said with a nod. I motioned to Mumo, Hadley, and Gio. "C'mon guys."

But it was maybe not an effective way to end the dispute. Blue turned and said something to his friends. Then, with determined looks in their eyes, they killed their bikes' engines and pumped their kickstands to the ground. They all climbed off and started coming toward us.

Next to me, Hadley stiffened a little. I did too, and that was all it took for sanity to rush in. Whatever extra cash they wanted from us, I knew it wasn't worth escalating things any further just to make my point.

"How much do you need?" I asked, clearly conveying my disgust with them.

"Two hundred shillings," Blue answered casually.

These men were willing to make themselves bullies of children, all for a gain of less than three bucks. And the worst part about it was how nonchalant they were, as if it was just another everyday business dealing to them.

With fire in my eyes, I counted out the money, then dropped it into his hand. "Here," I said, staring him down.

He closed his fist around the coins and nodded.

"Thank you," he said calmly, as he turned to leave.

He and his friends had won. They were bigger than us, they had ambushed us, and now they had our money and were going to get away with it. Still, I refused to let them have the last word.

"Understand," I announced, the words fuming out of me, "that this is the last time you'll *ever* get money from us. We will *never* hire you again. You just lost a *lot* of money on this."

After all his bravado, something in Blue's hard-hearted demeanor cracked, just slightly. I saw a new expression register on his face. He realized that he had been a fool, and I could tell that he instantly regretted it.

I guess I could have felt some kind of smug satisfaction, getting to see that. I didn't. Instead, I felt the weight of darkness. I was out just half the price of a cheap pizza, but three bucks in Kenya is a big deal, so it felt like a big deal to me too. It was easy enough to make me feel cheated, scorned, and used. Sadly, it was nowhere near the worst that could happen in Kenya. As our group was about to learn, only a few years earlier in Kibwezi things had gotten immeasurably darker and uglier.

CHAPTER 14

# School,
## *Interrupted*

In the early days of planning our trip to Kibwezi, Mumo had extended an invitation to us on behalf of his family. Along with his mother, Beatrice, he and his siblings wanted to host our Generation Next group for a meal at Beatrice's home, which was in a small town outside Kibwezi called Kathyaka, where Mumo grew up. We scheduled a Sunday afternoon visit, and I asked Mumo if there was anything in particular that we could bring as a gift for his mom. He told us that she was often cold at night and that she could use a blanket.

It's possible that our group, being so eager to meet Mumo and so grateful for his help and friendship, might have gone a little overboard on that bedding request. The five of us gathered up several warm, soft quilts from our homes, and after telling some of our friends about the cold nights at Beatrice's house, we received a few other blankets too. We brought them all with us to Kibwezi, where we showed them to Burgwin and asked if there was anything else we should add to the gift.

Burgwin told us that a family like Mumo's could probably make good use of maize flour, a Kenyan cooking staple. On that suggestion, we made a trip to the market and purchased a ninety-pound bag of it. Then, on the Sunday of our scheduled meeting, we all took a twenty-minute *boda-boda* ride across Kibwezi to say hello.

Several family members were already assembled outside Beatrice's home when we arrived: Beatrice, Mumo's three older brothers, his one older sister, two sisters-in-law, and two young nephews. We introduced ourselves and thanked Beatrice for hosting us, presenting her with the quilts and maize we had brought. She seemed thrilled to receive them, talking excitedly about how warm the quilts would be and how long the maize would last. She carefully chose a couple of the new quilts for her own home, then just as carefully distributed the others among the rest of her family.

From earlier conversations with Mumo, we knew that he and his siblings were all half siblings to one another. Each one of them had a different father, and none of those fathers had stuck around long term. An absentee dad is not at all uncommon in Kenya, unfortunately. Mumo's sister, Belta, lived with Beatrice and helped run the household. One brother, Nicholas, spent every day riding his bike to gather and bring back water for the family. Another brother, John, had an income from working at a school in Nairobi; he and his family lived next door to Beatrice and helped meet her ongoing needs. They all seemed glad to be taking care of one another.

They also insisted on being generous hosts to us. In the Kibwezi area, a typical daily diet consisted of rice, beans, some occasional vegetables, and a dish known as *ugali*, which is a starch that commonly serves as either a porridge or a cooked dough. Like most rural Kenyans, Mumo's family members rarely ate protein because it was costly. For the occasion of our visit, though, they had killed and prepared a whole chicken.

We ate our tasty meal outside under the shade of a small tree. Those who knew English and Swahili (Burgwin, John, and Mumo) were kept translating at high speeds while everybody got to know one another. Then after our meal, Mumo's family walked us all around the property to show us their homes.

Our first stop was Beatrice's hut. It was a round, one-room home, slightly bigger than some of the other homes we had seen, with mud walls and a thatched roof. We weren't invited inside, but we had been inside mud huts like hers before, so we had a good idea of what it would be like. The interior would be dim, due to the color of the walls and the lack of electricity. Bugs would be everywhere—they could burrow through the walls all day long, coming and going as they pleased. We knew from Mumo that Beatrice and Belta had beds, but if there was any other furniture in the house, it would likely be minimal.

Outside the hut was the kitchen and cooking area; our chicken dinner had been prepared there over an open fire. A little further beyond that was a chicken coop, now one hen short, thanks to our visit. Built out of long, thin branches, the coop was a circular enclosure of sticks tied tightly together, raised slightly above the ground and topped with its own thatched roof. A couple of the kids riled up the chickens, and everybody laughed.

Next we walked through the scrub brush a couple hundred yards to where John lived with his wife, Eunice, and their two children. For all intents and purposes, their place was pretty similar to Beatrice's, with one big difference. About twenty feet from the door of John and Eunice's hut stood an unfinished building. It had four plain mud walls, a couple of empty places for windows, and a hole where a door was meant to be.

"John, what's this building for?" my dad asked.

"Ah, yes," John said. "This was meant to be a school."

"Was?"

"Yes." He spoke thoughtfully, and we could all sense that there was a story lurking behind the words.

"You mean it's not going to be a school anymore?"

He sighed. "I do not know." Then he told us what had happened.

Several years earlier, a white missionary had come to Kibwezi with the dream of building a much-needed primary school for children in the area, and he and John became acquaintances. When John learned of the missionary's plans to build, he had offered his property as a site for the school. The two had made an agreement to move forward with that idea, and sometime later the missionary's school began taking shape. The four mud walls went up.

Then tragedy struck. In the middle of the project, the missionary was traveling in the region when he was approached by several men. They assumed that because he was white, he must be carrying a large amount of money. He assured them he wasn't, but they refused to believe him. Intent on getting his cash for themselves, they beat him savagely just so they could check his bags and turn his pockets inside-out.

The bandits went away with very little, exactly as they had been told they would, and the missionary later died from his injuries. As if the murder and the mourning weren't bad enough in themselves, Kathyaka also lost its hope of the school.

"I have thought about trying to complete it myself," John explained. At this, he inhaled a large breath and held it for a moment, as if he were going to say something hopeful. His hands were out in front of him, poised to make a gesture that would match the words. But then he sighed and dropped his arms to his sides. "It is too expensive for me," he told us, shaking his head. "The construction would take many years."

We shook our heads with him. Just hearing the story hit us like a blow; we couldn't imagine how it must have felt to have lived it.

Before our group got back on the road for Kambua that day, some of us ducked through the mud doorway of the empty school building and walked around inside for a while. We made pondering comments like, "It would have been a nice place for a school," and "So sad, isn't it?" Deep in thought, a bunch of white people hugging our arms against our chests, we grieved what might have been.

We would later discover that God wasn't finished with the story. It seemed that every time we turned around, he was planting more dreams in our hearts.

# CHAPTER 15

# NOT SO
## *Different*

N ear the end of our time in Kibwezi, we made a visit to St. Mary's School, an all-girls boarding school for secondary students where Burgwin's teenage daughter attended. It was too far away for *boda-bodas* to take us, so that morning Burgwin showed up at Kambua with a car and driver, and we all squeezed in for a ride. Making our way south down Mombasa Road, we were excited and lighthearted about the day ahead.

"The students go for three months," explained Burgwin; "then they are home again for three months; then it repeats. They are home for half the year and at school for half the year."

The area we were traveling in had a lot of trees, and the soil must have been good too, because there were plots of farmland all around us. We pulled up to a group of buildings that had all been painted to match one another: red exteriors with white-trimmed window frames and a white stripe running the length of the buildings just above the windows.

As we got out of the car, I noticed an open space beyond a couple of the buildings, diagonal to where we were standing.

"Hadley!" I exclaimed, signaling with my eyes toward the area. "They have courts!"

She looked over and saw what I had seen. In the middle of the school complex, there was a large yard that had been staked out in two different places to form side-by-side dirt rectangles, with boundaries marked by wooden pegs all the way around. A volleyball net had been strung across the middle of the smaller court, and on either edge of the larger one were two basketball hoops. The centers of both courts were decorated with the rich colors and quick movements of athletic young women squaring off in competition. This was where the roominess of the Kenyan school uniforms came in handy. From the waist down, each of the St. Mary's girls was wearing either a burgundy or teal-green skirt, billowy enough to dart around in and long enough to stay modest while running and jumping. Above the waist they wore brightly colored V-neck shirts with St. Mary's printed across the front.

Most of the athletes on both courts were barefoot, and as they played, they kicked up little puffs of chalky, red dirt. The tiny clouds held in the air for a few seconds before sticking to their feet and ankles. All that deep red earth clinging to dark brown skin was just one more striking contrast in an already vivid scene. As Hadley and I watched it unfolding, our eyes lit up. If I was the volleyball player back home in Branson, then Hadley was the basketball girl. We both loved to play and were missing our favorite sports while in Kenya, so all we had to do was look at those courts and we were chomping at the bit. We knew that we had potentially hours of competition ahead of us, and we couldn't wait to get started.

Yes, hours. Since our group had been aware that the St. Mary's students were boarding at the school full-time for the term, we had made arrangements to spend a good portion of our day there just hanging out. That sort of request would have been considered a waste of school resources and possibly an insult in the United States, but in Kenya it was not only perfectly appropriate, but it was also much appreciated. Three months away from your parents and siblings is a big deal to a teenager, and three months of constant school life is a big deal too. That's why officials at schools like St. Mary's are often more inclined to give their students special breaks for letting loose and having fun. If a bunch of random Americans appear, that's seen as an obvious opportunity presenting itself.

At St. Mary's, there was no grand announcement of our group's arrival and no presentation. We weren't there to be formal with the students; we were there to enjoy some time getting to know them. So almost as soon as we got out of our rented car, we all took off for the yard.

Two lines of young women, one for each sport, waited between the two courts for their turns to play. Hadley jumped into the basketball line, and I took the volleyball side, and soon we were rotating in and out of games and matches, making new friends, and swapping questions and answers with our fellow teenagers. We asked them where they were from, how far away it was from St. Mary's, and what activities they liked to do. They wanted to know who our favorite singers, actors, and actresses were. They asked if we had boyfriends, if we liked to sing, and whether or not we had met Justin Bieber. ("Not yet," we told them.)

It was a neat experience to hear from girls our age on the other

PLAYING VOLLEYBALL AT AN ALL-GIRLS SCHOOL WHERE
WE FOUND OUT THE NEED FOR HYGIENE KITS

side of the world. Our lives and theirs were worlds apart in so many ways, but we were obviously more the same than we were different. The more time I spent with them, the more I was sure of it. We all giggled about guys and relationships, we all got frustrated by our skirts sticking to our legs, we all preferred success on the court to failure, we all made small mistakes and big ones, and we were all trying to figure out how to best work together.

My dad came around to say that the Generation Next group would be leaving soon, and as we started saying good-bye, the St. Mary's girls abandoned their competitions to wish us well. They hugged us and told us to remember them, and we did the same. Then, in the middle of the farewells, suddenly Burgwin was standing in front of me with his typical huge grin and with an extremely tall young woman next to him.

"Riley, I did not want to leave without introducing you to my daughter and my daughter to you. This is Barbara. Barbara, this is Riley."

I don't know what I was expecting Burgwin's daughter to look and be like, but it wasn't like the person to whom I was being introduced. I guess I had assumed she would look like Burgwin and act like Burgwin, but where he seemed broad and sturdy, she was long and elegant. Where he was gregarious and extroverted, she obviously was not. Everything about this young woman said shy. Her shoulders were curved forward slightly, rounding out her spine. Her head dipped a little lower than it needed to. Her face wore a friendly expression but a bashful smile, and she had a kind of reluctance in her eyes that told me she was holding some things back. When she extended her hand to shake mine, she did it somewhat timidly, and when she spoke, her voice was quiet and a little airy.

"Hello, Riley. It's nice to meet you."

She was probably six inches taller than I, her life and culture were totally different from mine, and her skin was about as dark as

MY FIRST TIME TO MEET BARBARA AT SAINT MARY'S SCHOOL

mine was light. But although our circumstances and stories were different, we were cut from the same cloth. I was sure of it. When I looked at her, in many ways I felt like I was looking into a mirror.

"Hi, Barbara. It's really nice to meet you too."

At that point Burgwin left us, and for a little while Barbara and I worked at a conversation, both of us trying hard to come up with things to say. She thanked me for coming to her school. I told her that her dad was being a huge help to our group. Then there was silence for a minute, and I remembered that I had something to offer her. Reaching into my backpack, I pulled out one of the hemp necklaces I had made. It had a deep purple bead at the center, and I had been carrying it around for a while.

"Here," I said, holding it out to her. "I made this for you. It's a necklace."

She grinned nervously and took it from me. "It's very pretty. Thank you very much."

"You have to tie it on. I can do it for you if you want?"

"Okay, yes. Thank you."

Barbara turned away from me and bent her knees forward enough so I could reach up to her neck better.

"There," I said as I finished tying the necklace.

Instinctively she put her hand up to her throat to feel the braids of thread and the bead. "I like it."

We smiled at each other; then quickly we both looked toward the ground and shifted on our feet. That was when I saw it.

I had taken off my sandals to play volleyball more easily, and I hadn't put them back on yet. As we stood there together, neither of us was wearing shoes, and Kenya's red dust was stuck all over our skin. If you hadn't known that our lives were so different, and if you had tried to tell us apart by looking only at our feet, you might not have been able to do it. *Not so different.* That's what I was thinking as I hugged Barbara good-bye and went off to join the rest of the Generation Next group.

When I met up with my mom, Burgwin introduced us to the headmistress of St. Mary's. Turns out, it was a providential encounter.

# CHAPTER 16

# A DESPERATE
## *Need*

Mom and I got as comfortable as possible in the two chairs situated across from the headmistress and her desk. It was a typical office: papers stacked on top of files, a couple of certificates hanging on the wall. The room's one lone window had been flung open wide, but it wasn't letting in much breeze, so the place felt especially small and hot. Later I would wonder whether those conditions had made the headmistress seem even more fiery and looming than she actually was. Then again, maybe she gave off that impression all on her own.

"Thank you again for coming to our school," she said warmly. She closed the office door and then sat down at her desk, smiling. Even with her benevolent expression, she was an imposing figure. Her broad shoulders practically towered above her desk, and she leaned forward onto her elbows, already confident in what she was about to say.

"We are honored that you would come—here, please sign on this page." She slid the school's guest book across her desk to us.

"We've had a great time with your students," Mom replied.

"We really have," I added. "Thank you for being so kind and welcoming."

With that, Mom and I each signed our names and wrote the day's date. Then we smiled politely and waited, anticipating whatever the headmistress would have to say to us.

"You are most welcome. The girls and our staff are all thankful for your kindness."

There was a brief pause as we all looked at one another. Then the headmistress continued. "You know, it is very important that these girls get a good education. Here in Kenya an education affects a young woman's chances more than anything."

The pitch had begun. Mom and I settled a little deeper into our chairs. We were paying attention, and we were taking seriously what the headmistress was about to say to us, but I will admit that we were listening like people who had heard it before. At upward of seven other schools, we had heard as many of these speeches already. We figured the one at St. Mary's would be just like all the others: kids needing sponsors, kids needing surgeries, families needing cash. We had already gotten so used to schools requesting assistance that we almost didn't expect any of the particulars to surprise us anymore.

But the particulars put forth at this school were about to shock us. This headmistress was about to unearth a need and a request that was unlike anything we had yet encountered.

"Here at St. Mary's," she told us, "when the students come to school, they stay for three months at a time. This means that when they come, they must have everything they need for all three months. They must have their uniform, a notebook, writing supplies, and books. It is very expensive, very difficult to collect all of those things," she told us, "and for girls in a secondary school, it is even more expensive, because now they are old enough to have a period."

The headmistress went on to explain that at a school like hers, when each new season of classes begins, girls who have started having periods are required to have all the feminine hygiene supplies they will need for the duration of the term. Even if the student has a sponsor who is paying for her tuition and school fees, it's up to that student and her family or caretakers to produce three months' worth of sanitary napkins.

"Poor families in Kenya live on less than 100 shillings per day. Feminine products for three months can be equal to nearly a week's wages for these families." The headmistress shook her head. "Many of the girls cannot afford the hygiene supplies they need, but they are desperate to come to school. So what happens is that many of them make the choice to do desperate things."

That day we learned from the headmistress that it was not uncommon for teen girls to become prostitutes in the three months they spent away from school to earn the necessary funds for sanitary napkins. We also learned that some girls gave in to perverted requests from "uncles"—close relatives or other adult men in their lives—to have sex with them in exchange for money to buy hygiene supplies.

My stomach churned and knotted at the thought of it. I had become thoroughly uncomfortable in my chair, and beside me I could tell my mom had too. I felt a strong desire to leave the room for some fresh air and deep breaths. But first the headmistress had more to tell us. She was frowning and her eyes had darkened.

"There is very little contraception use in Kenya, especially in rural areas. This means that often, when a girl is selling her body, she becomes pregnant. Now she cannot go to school any longer. Or possibly she becomes infected with HIV." The headmistress shook her head and snorted with disgust. "What happens to the man? Nothing. His life does not change. But the girl has lost her chance to earn an education and a good job, or she has lost her health, or both. She is almost assured to live in poverty for life."

As the headmistress was speaking, I couldn't help but think of the young women we had spent the day with at St. Mary's. After even just a handful of hours with them, they had already begun etching themselves onto my heart. More than that, I had begun to see that we were the same. Like me, they were brimming with teenage angst and teenage promise. Like me, they dreamed about the future that stretched out in front of them. They wanted it to be hopeful and joyous. To think that anyone, let alone these girls or others like them, would ever have to face the kinds of choices that had just been described to us was sickening. I didn't want to think it could be real, and I didn't have any idea how to deal with it. Thankfully, though, I was sitting across from someone who was all-too-versed in the issue.

The headmistress was stretched nearly all the way across her desk now. Her demeanor was still as confident as ever, but her arms were out and her hands were up, pleading with us.

"This is a terrible problem in Kenya, and we need people who will help us fix it. Is there a way that your organization can help?" She looked us straight in the eyes. "Can you provide feminine hygiene products to some of this country's students?"

Mom and I glanced at each other for a moment before looking back at the headmistress. Then I spoke.

"If we came back to Kenya, it wouldn't be until next summer, because we would need a year to try to get supplies. But if we did come back, what kinds of hygiene products would the girls here need?"

"No, no, no," she waved her hands insistently. "Not at this school. The students at St. Mary's come from families that have more money. Many are still quite poor here, but I can tell you about other schools where the students have even less. I would tell you to help them first. But to answer your question, what the girls need most are sanitary napkins. There are other things that are also helpful, but the sanitary napkins are most needed."

Mom and I nodded in understanding. Seeing that, the head-mistress leaned back in her chair and gave a long exhale. I got the sense that she felt she had accomplished her duty with us that afternoon.

My mom closed the school guest book and pushed it back across the desk, and she and I stood up, preparing to leave.

"Thank you for telling us about this problem," I said to the headmistress. Then I said exactly what I had said at every other guest book session we had attended in Kibwezi: "We will consider all the things you've told us here today, and if there is anything we can do to help, we will do it."

As my mom and I walked out of St. Mary's to rejoin the rest of our group, we were both thinking the same thing. We would be returning to Kibwezi the following summer, and when we came back, we would bring as many maxi pads as we could carry!

*Our group* ON THE BUS

PUTTING TOGETHER *hygiene kits*

*Me playing* WITH STUDENTS AT PAMOJA

ME WITH A NEW MOTHER AT *the hospital*

GRACE TELLING THE KIDS
IT WAS OKAY TO TOUCH THE
*mzungu*

*Students* AT PAMOJA

*Children* AT A FEEDING PROGRAM

THE GIRLS PROUD OF THEIR *hygiene kits*

Me with one of the preemie triplets at Tenwek Hospital

Boys who received our *backpacks*

Breaking ground on *Pamoja*

PAMOJA KIDS SITTING IN THE FIRST DESK BUILT! THEY WERE SO *excited*.

SOME OF THE SWEET KIDS THAT ATTEND *Pamoja*

# CHAPTER 17

# A Little Bit of
## *Everything*

The decision happened almost effortlessly, but it came with one complication. The minute we decided to go back to Kenya for a third time, we knew we had several other choices yet to make. On top of the hygiene problem, we had encountered many other needs during our time in Kibwezi. Along with the girls in secondary school, we had met many other people who were facing big hardships. What were we going to do about all of them?

One of my family's ongoing jokes is that I'm the vision caster for Generation Next. What they mean is that I have a knack for dreaming up ideas while overlooking details. In those early years in Kenya, more than once I got my heart set on a splashy end goal without thoroughly considering if there was a workable plan to reach it. That was an easy trap to fall into, though, and not just for me. After becoming aware of needs that seem endless, it's hard to keep from trying to address everything.

A case in point: when we decided to help provide feminine products for teen girls, we were prompted to take a second look at some other service options too. We would definitely be collecting and delivering hygiene supplies, but along with that, what other projects could we take on? Over time I've learned a lot of lessons on how to be a responsible and discerning and strategic planner.

The first thing we considered was school supplies. That was the need that had brought us back to Kenya a second time, and we wanted to stick with it in one way or another. We had personally seen thousands of kids who lacked basic educational tools, so we knew firsthand that two hundred backpacks had barely scratched the surface. But what should a second year of collection and delivery look like?

The second big need we were thinking about was the school on John and Eunice's property started by the missionary who had been murdered. For the building to be ready for use, several layers of bricks had to be added to the walls, trusses and a roof had to be put on, concrete flooring had to be laid, and a kind of mud stucco-type effect had to be applied to all the walls, with paint as a seal on top of that. Then basic supplies like a chalkboard and desks would need to be purchased and brought in, not to mention a teacher and students. Had God brought our Generation Next team to that school for a reason? Did he want us to do something there?

The third big need on our minds was the problem of medical expenses. We were beginning to understand why hospitals like Tenwek existed in Kenya. The combination of high disease levels and extreme poverty was taking a staggering toll. Hospital stays were practically inevitable in the life of a family, but medical bills from a hospital stay were often impossible for them to pay off. Until the country's economy could make a major upswing, that wasn't going to change. Countless people in Kibwezi needed money to cover their past medical expenses, and countless more needed medical services made available to them at a more affordable rate, ideally free. What, if anything, could our group do to help with that?

We weighed our options. We prayed for direction. We did some preliminary research of costs and fees. Then we came to a decision about year three: we would deliver feminine hygiene products to teen girls, and we would adopt the missionary's school project as our own. As for the medical needs and hospital bills, we simply weren't equipped to take them on. We knew that since none of us was medically trained, our only way to help would be to dole out cash, and that ran the risk of getting extremely complicated. It wasn't the safest idea in the world to carry around large amounts of money in rural Kenya, and even if it had been, that plan would have left us trying to figure out who should be helped and who should be turned away. How do you even begin to do that?

We wanted to commit to only the projects we could do well, and we didn't want to stretch ourselves or our resources too thin. Between the school building and the sanitary napkins plan, we had more than enough for a small group to handle, and that was just considering the manpower side of things. The financial aspect was going to be big too. Even without taking on medical expenses or services, we were going to need to raise several thousand dollars over the next year. John and Eunice had estimated that the school's remaining construction costs would amount to about 500,000 Kenyan shillings, or $5,000. We also wanted to be prepared to employ a teacher for a year and provide school uniforms for all fifty would-be students. That would cost an additional $1,500 or so. The number of school and hygiene items we would need to collect was in the thousands too. And on top of all that, we would need to bring in enough money to fly our Generation Next team over to Kenya to get the work done.

The price tag for all we wanted to accomplish was going to be a big hike compared to each of our previous trips. Still, we had been learning that if God is leading, then he sees things through and provides what is needed. Over the course of just two years, many of our friends and family members had come to care a lot about our work with Generation Next, and many of them had contributed to our previous trips. Maybe some of them would be interested in giving again or giving more. Or maybe this year God would provide new relationships that would result in supplies and support. Whatever the case, our plan was set. At least, we thought it was.

We began digging into logistics, and in the process we called Robin to reconnect. After sharing some highlights from our first trip to Kibwezi and thanking her again for her help, we told her that we were planning to return to the area, and why. She immediately got excited.

"That's wonderful! Wow, really great. Then, in that case, I have an idea for you. I think I mentioned to you before that Namba is trying to start up a children's home, right?"

"Yeah, you did. That's so exciting!"

"We think so too. Over the past several years, we've been building Namba House while waiting to get approval for having children live here. It's in good enough shape now, but we might not have kids in it until next winter, so over the summer we're planning to host a medical clinic here. I'm already lining up a team of Kenyan physicians, and we're in the process of arranging for medical supplies too. We're mostly set, but we can always use more volunteers for basic tasks during the clinic, like checking people in and taking vital signs. And it wouldn't hurt for us to have a little more money for medical supplies either. If you think Generation Next would be interested in partnering with us for the clinic at Namba House, I'd love to talk about making that happen."

Not long after that call, Generation Next had committed to hygiene products, the missionary's school and supplies, and a multiple-day medical clinic. It was going to be a little bit of everything, and we would need a lot of support to accomplish it all.

Several times a week, in several kinds of ways, we worked at rounding up donations for our second trip to Kibwezi.

"Would you be able to donate any toothbrushes or toothpaste for the hygiene kits we're putting together?"

"Would you like to buy a bracelet to help us bring school supplies to kids in Africa?"

"Would your church be willing to host a presentation from our team?"

"Would you consider contributing to Generation Next in support of our upcoming projects in Kenya?"

That third year, I'd guess that both my mom and I spent ten to fifteen hours every week working toward our next trip. Between the two of us, we were putting in enough hours for a legitimate part-time job. It was a big change, one that none of us would have predicted. We had been just a few family members and some friends with a mission, to bring school supplies to kids in Africa. Toward the end of our second year's work, even the fact that we had a formal nonprofit organization attached to us had seemed a little silly at times. From our perspective, Generation Next was mostly just a tax-exempt number that we could use for securing donations. We hadn't been looking to grow into an organization. We hadn't been looking to have others come along with us on trips or to keep returning to Kenya ourselves either. We had only wanted to help kids in Africa. But even though we hadn't been looking for growth as an organization, the ways we were expanding were beginning to come in handy.

# CHAPTER 18

# Generosity

As our next trip to Kenya neared, once again my mom, dad, and I were looking forward to more than just our own adventure. My brother Cameron's youth basketball coach, Tyler, had heard about Generation Next and, along with his new fiancée, Dorothy, had asked to serve with us that summer. We were also going to be joined by Graham, another high school student our family had known for years and whom I had recently started dating. We had developed a great group dynamic, which was wonderful. Still, almost equally important was that there were *six* of us—more than ever before, which, for one, meant there were more of us invested in collecting supplies and donations. Each of us was able to reach out to our own networks to share about the needs in Kibwezi and to request support for the work that Generation Next would be doing. My parents put up a sign at the print shop they owned and pointed it out to their best customers. I braided hemp necklaces and sold them. Tyler talked it up to his team. And Graham helped serve lunch at his family's eatery to raise the funds to come along. Along with that, having six people meant we could also up our suitcase allotment, which meant a lot more supplies could come with us.

Then there was that tax-exempt number of ours, which had already proven to be a game changer. Our ability to request and receive contributions had increased dramatically when we were granted nonprofit status. People took us more seriously, businesses were quicker to support our work, and churches were more willing to partner with us. Little by little, and sometimes lots by lots, Branson and other local communities were helping us prepare to meet needs in Kibwezi. Once again my family had needed to clear out our garage so it could be used as a staging area.

On top of gathering school supplies for fifty-plus children at the missionary's school, our group had set a goal to put together two hundred hygiene kits for teen girls. Our plan was that the kits would include not just sanitary napkins but a number of other personal care items as well. We were aiming for bar soap, hand sanitizer, a toothbrush and toothpaste, dental floss, laundry detergent, some panty liners, and an extra pair of panties. (Most kids and teens in Kenya own only one pair of underwear, if that, and considering feminine hygiene needs, we figured girls would appreciate a spare.)

When it came to a few local businesses, we hit the jackpot in terms of receiving donated supplies. On one trip to a local spa and skin care store, we asked about potential donations, and they "just happened" to have several boxes of hand sanitizer that they were waiting to give away. Another area nonprofit had requested the items but had never showed to pick them up, so the store passed them on to us. I was learning to appreciate all the things that "just happened." They were "just happening" to us a lot.

I was also developing a deeper appreciation for my local dentists. In the beginning of our supply collection, we visited a few dental offices to ask for oral hygiene products. I don't know why I expected them to turn us down, but I did. Probably I had gotten a little used to the typical pattern of rejection: only some people were interested in supporting us, not everybody. But that wasn't the case with Branson's dentists. Every single one of the dentists we approached was happy to donate supplies. We came away with more toothpaste, toothbrushes, and floss than we would have thought possible, and we scratched oral care items off our "still needed" list right away.

As for most of the other necessary supplies, our area churches came through in a big way. About twice a month my family and I would visit a new congregation that had agreed to support Generation Next that year. Sometime during the service, I'd be given the opportunity to deliver a presentation, which I would nervously do.

After each of my presentations, a church leader would respond by encouraging everyone to give, pointing them to a table in the lobby where I'd be at the end of the service. There would always be a line of people at our table looking to help us out. Most of the churches would then continue to collect items for us in their own lobbies or offices so people could contribute as conveniently as possible.

By late spring the evidence of people's generosity was all over our garage. Our friends, family, and community members had donated thousands of items for Kibwezi, as well as made financial contributions for construction, travel, and the medical clinic. We were overwhelmed by the support and by God's provision. Nevertheless, we would soon be on our knees asking him to come through even more.

# CHAPTER 19

# A WINK AND A

## *Grin*

One Friday afternoon, with our trip to Kenya just a few weeks away, my mom and I went out to the garage to get a head start on packing. On the one hand, we knew we were in for a fun time. On the other hand, we were aware it was going to be highly frustrating. The place was stuffed beyond belief. On one side, we had box after box full of markers, crayons, scissors, pencils, and pencil sharpeners. Down the middle, folding tables sat loaded with piles of Bibles and notebooks. On the other side, we had bins full of nearly everything we needed for the hygiene kits.

Mom and I were ecstatic about our haul, and it was a joy to sift through everything. Even so, as we began sorting the donated items and packing them into our totes and suitcases, we became painfully aware that something important was missing: maxi pads. People simply hadn't donated them, and we had a pretty good idea why.

For starters, most people would feel much more comfortable putting a few hundred pencils on the conveyor belt at Target than they would putting down multiple giant packages of maxi pads. That's the simple truth of it. Periods and period products aren't nearly the taboo subject in the States that they are in Kenya, but

Our garage with all the school supplies collected from Branson School District

even in America we would find it strange to go shouting "menstruation" from the rooftops. We keep our pads and tampons hidden in drawers and cupboards and in little zippered pouches in our backpacks and purses. We take them to bathrooms with us as discreetly as possible. And if we see them on a list of supplies that could be donated for Kenya, we're more likely to donate another kind of item instead, leaving the pads to someone else.

Along with that, sanitary napkins are expensive. As far as our Generation Next team could tell, that seemed to be a cross-cultural phenomenon, because pads are almost exactly the same price in the United States as they are in Kenya. And while that cost seems more affordable for Westerners because our household incomes are much higher, it's still a relatively high price compared to most school supplies. That's especially the case when you consider how inherently disposable pads are by design. Since sanitary napkins are single-use, and since a girl will probably use several of them in a day for several days each month, that's a steep bill compared to pens and pencils. Nearly every other item we collect to give away in Kenya is something that will cost just a fraction of a penny per day over the course of time, but maxi pads, which cost between ten and fifty cents apiece, can cost as much as $1.50 per girl per month. That's five cents every day, just on sanitary napkins. The price of pads easily eclipses the price of any other item a student might need.

We didn't know of any way we could get the pads that were so desperately needed. Generation Next was about as small as a nonprofit can get. We didn't have regular financial contributors or a steady source of income, and we barely had any money in the bank. We had always simply asked people to give supplies, and people's response had been almost entirely sufficient. Almost. As an organization we didn't have the necessary funds to go out and buy a couple thousand maxi pads, and as a family we didn't either. One store had given us a $50 gift card, which would buy us only eight large packs of pads—nowhere close to what we would need if we were going to pass out hygiene kits to entire schools.

On one of the tables in our garage, we had two hundred paper gift bags that were supposed to become our hygiene kits. They were big enough to hold all the health and sanitary items we had been collecting for the girls, and we had planned to pass out one to each student. But without the sanitary napkins, I wondered if they would be of much use at all.

I stood in the middle of our garage and looked around for a minute. "Hey, Mom?" I said. "Can I talk something through with you?"

She was in the middle of packing crayons into a suitcase. "Sure, honey."

I took a deep breath. Then I said what I'd been hoping for a long time that I wouldn't have to say about any of our efforts.

"I don't think we can do the hygiene kits this year if we don't get any pads."

"You'd really consider not doing the kits at all? Are you sure?"

"Yeah, I think so. Not without pads. They're the main reason why we wanted to do this in the first place."

My mom sighed. "I know. Man, I was praying we wouldn't have to start thinking like this."

"Me too." I bit the inside of my lip. Mom and I both surveyed our piles of supplies. Then after a minute or so, she spoke up.

"Okay, well, we only have a couple of weeks left before we leave. If nothing else comes in, it sounds like a wise decision to not do the kits. In the meantime, we can keep praying and keep trying to think of something. Sound good?"

So we put the conversation to rest and got back to packing. Still, as we filled up the different totes and suitcases around us, both of us stayed deep in thought. We had been looking forward to delivering hygiene kits for nearly a year, so it was tough to realize that it probably wasn't going to happen. Knowing that the girls in Kibwezi needed hygiene items so badly, we were both having a difficult time accepting that they likely weren't going to get them.

About a half hour later, we were still hard at work in the garage when my mom's phone rang. She picked it up, looked at the caller ID, and smiled. "It's Grandma," she told me, swiping the screen to accept the call. It was nothing unusual for my grandma to call our family. We probably spoke with her at least once a week, if not more. Talking with her was an ordinary part of our life. But on this day, my grandma's call would turn out to be extraordinary.

"Hi," my mom said to Grandma. "I've got you on speaker."

"Okay, great. I'm glad you're both there, because I'm calling about something for Generation Next. I was at work today, and I think maybe I have something that could help you."

Grandma was great at coming up with creative solutions to

help the ministry, and she worked as a substitute nurse at a school a few hours away, so she often had good ideas about supplies.

"We're all ears," my mom told her.

"Well, it's only if you still need sanitary napkins for your trip. I'm at the office, and we just got three complimentary cases of sanitary napkins shipped in. We're already so stocked up we'll never use these. Would you have room—"

I didn't even let her finish. "Yes! Yes! We'll take them. We want them all!"

Grandma chuckled. "Okay, well that was easy."

"Mom and I were just talking about how we still need pads for the hygiene kits, Grandma."

"Oh, perfect! Then it helps everybody. I'll clear them out of the office, and we can plan a time to meet in the next few days so that I can get them to you."

I looked over at my mom and gave her a huge smile, but she gave me just a quick one back. I could see her wheels turning.

"Is it normal for schools to get big shipments of pads and not use them?" asked my mom.

"I would guess that for all the middle schools and high schools, yes," Grandma replied.

Mom looked at me and raised her eyebrows. "Okay. In that case, would you mind if we hang up with you so we can call Riley's high school?"

With that, the three of us said our good-byes, and my mom placed the call. After being connected with the school nurse, she gave a quick overview of what we were doing in Kibwezi, including why we were looking for maxi pads.

"By any chance, does the high school have extra pads lying around that it won't need?"

As a matter of fact, the nurse told her, they had just received a shipment of nine cases that day. Nine cases! And they didn't need any of them. So, after months and months of trying to track down what we needed and deciding that the hygiene kits probably weren't going to happen, God came through with twelve cases of maxi pads in less than thirty minutes! It was enough for two hundred hygiene kits, but I shouldn't have been surprised by that one bit. Providing a bunch of sanitary napkins all at once is just the sort of thing that God had pulled off time and again for Generation Next. He came through with exactly what we needed, at exactly the right time, not a moment too late or too soon.

Over time this sort of thing has become an almost unmistakable pattern. We'll run up against a wall with a need that has somehow begun to feel impossible to meet. Then we'll consider every solution we can think of on our own until we've exhausted every alternative. Finally, we'll toss up our hands in surrender, accepting that what we wanted to happen is simply not going to happen after all. Then God, who has been in control all along, whips through and changes everything in an instant. Suddenly the undoable thing is done. What was out of the question is remarkably in.

Even though God had proven himself to me many times by now, I had gotten caught up in the circumstances directly in front of me and had forgotten that God is bigger than them all. I had believed he was leading us to deliver hygiene kits, but I had doubted his ability to provide when he leads. His response to my doubt wasn't punishment; it was unmistakable grace. You could even say it was humor: he made giant boxes of maxi pads materialize out of thin air! These are the times when God leaves no room for cynicism about whether or not the credit belongs to him.

I guess, though, that it would still be possible to doubt his goodness, even in something as obvious as this. In fact, I'm sure there are some who would assert that if God is in a story like this at all, then he's just playing some kind of disturbed, twisted puppet game. That he must get some kind of perverse pleasure out of watching people squirm.

Here is another way to read it: the maker of all things is finding ways to make himself known to those he has made. Maybe if I lived in a place like Kenya and had to wake up every day wondering whether I'd have enough to eat and drink, and maybe if I had to wonder those same things about everyone I loved, then it wouldn't take grand, blatant gestures for me to appreciate God's provision. Maybe if I had a little less of what I need, then I would remember a little more how much I need him. Maybe if I trusted him to give me what I lack, he wouldn't have to give me such repeated reminders that I can trust him.

It would be perfectly within God's right to blast me every single time I forget his power or overlook his generosity to me. Instead, just when I understand once again how much I need him, he is there. He shows up, with a wink and a grin, so I won't miss the miracle.

# CHAPTER 20

# HEALING AND
*Hope*

After arriving in Kibwezi in 2012 and seeing the progress that had been made at Namba House, we could see why Robin had decided that it would be a perfect place for a community-wide medical clinic. It was massive by Kenyan standards: it had two stories with multiple rooms downstairs and a two-bedroom apartment upstairs, and the main floor was so big that it had a giant central area plus a pair of separate wings.

Along with Robin and her team, we prepared for the clinic by setting up a basic reception table at the property's gate, a waiting area just outside the building, a large intake room just inside, private exam rooms beyond that, and lastly, a pharmacy where all the prescribed medicines and vitamins would be kept. Advertisement for the clinic had been all verbal, with mostly Burgwin and other local social workers spreading the word, and it had been effective. We opened the clinic doors early one Tuesday morning, and by then a long line had already been forming.

Aside from helping provide vitamins and medicines for the clinic, our Generation Next team largely took over the waiting area and intake roles. A couple of us helped monitor the pace of things, ushering people from the outside of the building to the inside as spaces opened up. The rest of us had been put in charge of individual intake stations. Armed with a basic blood pressure gauge and pulse oximeter each, we took and recorded vitals for every patient who came through the clinic.

Over the course of three long workdays, our team of doctors and volunteers saw and treated more than thirteen hundred patients, averaging more than four hundred per day. To put that in context, that number was quadruple as many patients as one Branson Emergency Room was averaging in a twenty-four-hour period. Our services ran the gamut too, from providing free malaria and HIV testing, to pulling cockroaches out of ears and treating scorpion stings, to treating cuts and burns.

On our fourth day we delivered all two hundred hygiene kits to three different girls' schools in Kibwezi. The evening before at Kambua Guest House, we had packed all the hygiene items into pastel-colored gift bags, each one with a little tag on it that said, "For Girls Only." It was a thrill seeing those kits all ready for delivery, and we weren't the only ones who thought so.

MOM, DAD, AND ME AFTER HOSTING A MEDICAL CLINIC IN KIBWEZI

Burgwin's daughter Barbara, whom I had met after playing volleyball the year before, had become a great friend to me. We had been emailing back and forth regularly, and we had been looking forward to seeing each other again during our second trip. Barbara had been permitted to take the day off of school to help us deliver hygiene kits, so that morning when Burgwin came to get us with a rented car, she was with him. After big hugs with me and shy hugs with everybody else, Barbara helped our group load into the car with the kits, and we all took off for our special delivery.

At each of the schools, we were given a sweet reception, typically some welcoming remarks from an official, and then a song or two featuring the students. After that we gathered all the teen girls together in a room so we could introduce the kits and explain how to use them. The students at one of the schools had never seen white people in person before, let alone a package of dental floss, so we wanted to make sure they understood their new products before trying to use them.

THE FIRST GIRLS TO RECEIVE A HYGIENE KIT FROM GENERATION NEXT

A group of girls who came to our hygiene day at Kambua guest house

Standing at the front of the room with a hygiene kit in hand and a translator at my side, I took out the items one by one and described what the girls would be receiving that day. Since they had already learned English in school, they mostly understood what I was saying, but at times when things got technical, the translator would elaborate in Swahili or a mother tongue. (Imagine trying to learn the difference between bar soap and hand sanitizer in your second or third language and you'll get the picture.)

The girls could not wait to get their hands on the kits. At all three schools, when I pulled out a travel-size tube of toothpaste from my sample hygiene kit, some of the girls gasped audibly with disbelief. Others of them clapped their hands over their mouths with glee. It would have warmed the hearts of all those generous Branson dentists, for sure.

As for the maxi pad I held up on display, the students responded to it with snickers and giggles at first, as might be expected in any audience of teenagers anywhere. But when the translator and I explained that there were fifteen of them in each hygiene kit, we heard a collective intake of breath. A supply like that was gold to those girls!

After everything had been spelled out, our Generation Next team ceremoniously passed out a kit to each girl. As a group, the students thanked us profusely: applause, hugs, kind words. You might have thought we had changed their lives forever.

Even so, in the middle of the ruckus, I couldn't help but have a sense of disquiet about the whole thing. Fifteen pads. Just fifteen. As we pulled away from the last school that day, I turned to my mom and said, "Well, those pads will take care of them for about a month. Then what are they gonna do?"

None of us had any idea about that, but I knew what *I* wanted to do. I wanted to come back to Kibwezi with more hygiene products just as soon as I could.

CHAPTER 21

# The Dedication

We didn't even come close to finishing the elementary school in Kathyaka during that trip. When we left, there were still only holes where doors and windows were meant to be. The concrete flooring hadn't been installed either, and nearly all the brick walls still needed to be sealed with a mortar solution, not to mention primed and painted.

We had made what we thought was a simple plan for completing the school, which we had named Pamoja ("together"). Each day we spent on the construction site, we would hire several workers from in town to help with the building. Mumo, John, and Burgwin had all volunteered their time and work too, which meant that every day we would have upward of a dozen people at the schoolhouse. We had designated nearly two weeks to complete the work, and with as many people as we had, we figured that time frame was on the generous side. There would be enough manpower to get things done and plenty of wiggle room for surprises, we thought.

What we hadn't accounted for, though, were the donkeys.

In the United States, if you order a shipment of supplies for a project and specify that you need it to arrive by a certain day and a certain time, you can reasonably expect that it will. That's just how business and commerce work here. Companies pride themselves on timely deliveries, and in general, delays aren't easily tolerated.

CONSTRUCTION ON OUR SCHOOL, PAMOJA

Everybody knows that getting a job done right requires having the materials on hand from the start, so everybody makes sure that happens.

Not so in Kathyaka. There the process was: John went to town to order our supplies on an as-needed basis, and after the order was made, the supplies were delivered to the construction site by a team of donkeys. There weren't more desirable options: either we could buy all our construction supplies at once and risk leaving them lying around unattended overnight, or we had to deal with the donkey situation. We figured we would rather take our chances with the pack animals.

In other words, every day at the school site, we waited. And waited. After doing whatever we could to get things ready for that day's labor, whether collecting trash, digging up invasive plants, or smoothing out the dirt floor inside the building, we would soon run out of prep work and start scanning the horizon for our donkey team. We would fill our time playing with John and Eunice's kids, getting to know our hired workers, journaling, and reapplying sunscreen. Then when the donkey cart finally brought us the bricks or bags of cement we had ordered, we did all the constructing we could in whatever daylight hours remained. But it just wasn't enough.

The following summer, when we made our fourth trip to Kenya, finishing the school in Kathyaka was our top priority. Keeping in mind donkey time, we knew completion wouldn't be fast, but in due time the day of our grand opening arrived.

I woke up ready to jump out of my bed but realized I was tangled in my mosquito net . . . again. Once I detangled my limbs, I bounced out of bed, slid on my T-shirt, and pulled up my skirt until the hem was just skimming my feet. I stepped outside and walked to the dining room to join everyone for eggs, fresh fruit, and toast to start off our big day. Then we heard the roar of engines as one . . . two . . . three . . . and four *boda-bodas* pulled in to pick us up. We grabbed school supplies, uniforms, and bags of suckers, and off we went.

As we pulled up to the school, we were greeted by little squeals and arms tugging at our clothes. Fifty little faces. Fifty toothy

PUTTING THE FINISHING TOUCHES ON PAMOJA

grins. One hundred sweet little hands reaching up for hugs. I was surprised to see about fifty adults sitting in plastic lawn chairs in the shape of a crescent. I smiled and waved to them as they watched me walk over to John and Eunice's house, about twenty feet from the school. We had hired Eunice as the teacher, and she was remarkably gifted.

We started the day by pulling all the girls into Eunice's little house and dressing them in their new uniforms. I also had a uniform made to match theirs, so I went into a separate room and slid my uniform on too. When I came out I wasn't surprised to hear a burst of giggles at the big white girl being dressed just like them. We then lined up all the girls to march up to the school so they could sit in their new desks and bask in their new classroom. As we emerged from the house, I heard an even louder burst of laughter from all the parents at seeing the white girl dressed in Kenyan clothes.

Soon the boys joined us, dressed in their own uniforms, with Graham in tow, dressed just like them. When everyone was seated, we had a quick photo shoot, and then we went back outside to play. We played soccer and cuddled babies while we waited on lunch to be prepared. Once the meal was served, we had everyone gather around the front of the school for a little ceremony.

John was first up, since he had been instrumental in our dream for this project. He thanked us for our hard work on the school and for seeing something in it besides an empty, broken building, abandoned after a tragic death. Then he invited me to formally open Pamoja.

I walked to the front of the group of one hundred or so people, feeling their eyes on me. The years of visiting Kenyan schools had made me somewhat used to giving speeches, but my jitters about talking in front of people still hadn't gone away. I took a deep breath. If any speech was important, this one was.

"It is so exciting to share such a special day with all of you," I began. Then I looked to the Kenyan parents and addressed them directly. "Thank you for your beautiful children." I went on to express our team's hopes that an education would be the start of a bright future for Pamoja's kids, and that as they got older God would help guide them, protecting their hearts and keeping them safe. I thanked them for their support and for allowing us to reach out to their kids.

With that I turned to the school building behind me, where a thin sheet had been hung over the outside wall just next to the classroom door. I slid the sheet aside to reveal a special message painted in black:

> Building dedicated by
> Generation Next
> Riley Banks
> 20th June, 2013

We had prepared a shallow dish of black paint for that

We did it!

moment. As I read the message out loud to the group, I dipped my hand in the paint and then pressed it onto the wall, leaving my personal mark—my handprint on the entrance to the school. That silhouette mimicked Generation Next's logo, which is the shape of a hand with an outline of Africa inside it. It reminded us of the vision we'd had from the beginning: that ordinary people can have an extraordinary impact, one life at a time. That dream had carried us through several big twists and turns, but the premise had always stayed the same. We wanted to show God's love by providing for basic needs. If we could provide some kind of rescue in the name of Christ to kids in Kenya, even in small ways, then maybe one day those kids would more fully understand that Christ is the source of all rescue. Maybe they would seek him and be forever changed. And maybe that change in them would make a difference in their community. Maybe it would be like the drop at the center of a ripple effect: loved by God, they would love their neighbors in a rescuing way. Maybe this generation of kids in Kenya would change everything. Or maybe what we had done so far was the

ME WITH ALL THE KIDS OF PAMOJA AT THE GRAND OPENING

extent of it, and we had simply been given the privilege of throwing starfish back into the ocean.

When we were finished with the ceremony, I didn't know how to express the utter joy I felt, besides with my huge smile and the little giggles that bubbled out. I wanted to give these kids a place to go to be kids, to have fun, and to be safe as they learned. I not only wanted to do all that for these kids, but I wanted to come home and be able to tell this amazing story to hundreds of people so they would be inspired to pursue their own dreams.

As we headed back to Nairobi for our trip home a few days later, my mind was spinning and my heart was full—and a little troubled too. Before going to Kenya, everything I knew was arguably comfortable and full. I never had anything too serious to be worried about. No part of my life ever felt like it was "on the line," at least no more than life would be for any other preteen in suburban, middle-class America. That was the only kind of living I knew, and that was the only kind any of my friends knew too: cozy and secure.

And shallow, perhaps. And maybe a little too tame.

By contrast, in Kenya I saw major concerns everywhere. Families had to scrape by every day, sometimes just to have one meal in their bellies before going to bed at night. A single hospital bill—and in Kenya, you can catch disease simply by drinking water—could have a years-long crippling effect on a family's financial resources. Some children were unable to go to school because they had to walk miles every day, fetching water and bringing it home. Toddlers commonly suffered terrible burns from stumbling into open cooking fires. Young women were willing to do almost anything, sickeningly so, just to have the money they needed to go to school. An education seemed like their only chance to earn a good living and break the hold that poverty would otherwise have on their future.

In other words, in Kenya I saw people living their lives as if nearly everything was on the line. I saw them dreaming dreams that seemed far out of reach, taking big risks on a regular basis. Most strikingly, I saw the depth of faith demonstrated by Christians in Kenya—Christians who had God and little else. These people looked to God for *everything*. They trusted him day in and day out for food on the table, clothes on their backs, safety on the road, relief from financial strain, healing from disease—you name it.

And they were happy. They were *so happy*. I had never seen joy and faith that went so deep, and that faith was stunningly beautiful to me. It defied my spiritual understanding at that point and was beginning to change my outlook on pretty much everything. Seeing people giving everything they have to a cause leaves an impression. When along with that you see people trusting God for all they need, you may feel a need to do a reality check, which may reveal flimsy faith and superficial beliefs. On the best days, it will make you want to root out those things completely.

Here is what I saw when I looked at myself pre-Kenya: I saw that I could be lazy, more prone to relax and skate through life than to appreciate the value of hard work. And I saw that I didn't *really* understand how hard work could actually be. I had never had to labor for my own food, clothes, schooling, medical treatments, or housing, and I had certainly never done so for others. I saw how ungrateful I was for all the *stuff* in my life, considering how little my friends in Kenya owned. I saw how obnoxious it seemed that I expected to always have enough of everything. I saw how ridiculous it was that I had never once looked around and realized that I was so, so rich.

More than anything else, though, I saw that I didn't rely on God like I could. The dreams I dreamed pre-Kenya had been big enough for me to handle on my own—I rarely dreamed in a way that *needed* him. And there was hardly any urgency in the way I thought about sharing my faith with others. I acted like both they and I had all the time in the world.

I didn't. They didn't. We don't.

In the time I'd spent in Kenya so far, I knew I'd become bolder and more daring, braver and more trusting. My faith had been fortified. My dreams had expanded exponentially, and they had become big enough that I knew I couldn't reach them on my own. None of this was to my credit; the courage and reliance I saw in my life were still minuscule compared to what my Kenyan friends exhibited on a regular basis. They helped me see God's goodness and provision for what they are. They inspired gratitude and joy, not to mention flashes of grit and spunk, in me.

Still, there was no way for me to anticipate the kind of faith that would be required of me after I got home. I was in for the shock of my life.

CHAPTER 22

# SOMETHING'S
## *Missing*

B ranson, Missouri, late September, on my lunch hour. As I'd done every other school day recently during the break between classes my junior year, I pulled out my phone to text my mom one question: **DID YOU FIND OUT?**

Today, finally, her answer was different.

> YEP. I FOUND OUT.
>
> **TELL ME!!**
>
> IT'S NOT SOMETHING WE CAN TEXT ABOUT.
>
> LET'S TALK RIGHT AFTER SCHOOL.
>
> DON'T WORRY. LOVE YOU.

For the rest of the day, I tried not to let my MRI results distract me completely. I went to my next couple of classes and tried to focus on schoolwork. After that I went to volleyball practice and tried to focus on the sport. Occasionally I was able to concentrate for a few minutes on the task at hand—a math problem, a science quiz, a quick block or a strong serve—but mostly I spent the afternoon worrying and praying.

I'd had the MRI a couple of weeks earlier. It had been the third in a string of unexpected and less-than-pleasant medical events, including an ER visit for chest pains and dizziness, which revealed an extra flap on my heart. I'd also been having significant back pain, which turns out was the result of four bulging disks. Then there was the ultrasound, which had gone badly, hence the need for the follow-up MRI.

Leading up to all of this was a visit with Dr. Allison, prompted by my mom's concern over my symptoms, as well as the fact that at the age of sixteen, I hadn't yet had a monthly period.

"Well, Riley," she'd said with a reassuring smile, "I'm pretty confident we'll find out that your reproductive system is normal and healthy, but I'm going to order an ultrasound on your lower abdomen just to be sure. It sounds like you've had enough medical mysteries already, so let's get a solid conclusion on this one, okay?"

The recommendation of a new test made my mom sigh with relief, but I was exasperated. It seemed unnecessary to jump through yet another hoop just to have someone give me the definitive diagnosis of "late bloomer."

I'd gone into my ultrasound expecting a routine procedure—just a handful of radiology pictures and then Mom and I would be on our way. It hadn't occurred to me that there would be any reason to leave feeling concerned. But from the beginning, nothing about that ultrasound was routine.

First, the tech had informed me that my bladder wasn't full enough for her to see what she needed to see. We paused the test, and I drank a bottle of water, giving it time to work its way through my system. Back on the sterile hospital paper an hour later, with a new squirt of cold gel on my stomach, I was informed that now my bladder was *too* full for the tech to see what she needed to see. She instructed me to "slightly empty" my bladder—try that sometime just for kicks—and we started over again.

The third time around, I lay in the exam room for another hour as the tech moved her probe all over my lower abdomen. She pushed and prodded against my skin so forcefully that for a while I wondered if she was testing how much it would take for me to wet my pants. But she hadn't taken her eyes off the computer monitor in front of her, and at the half-hour mark, she began to chew the inside of her cheek. With a furrowed brow, she'd said, "I'm just not seeing what I'm supposed to see."

She said it more than once, several times. Every time those words bounced around the dim, sterile room, they seemed more ominous. My eyes were darting around faster and faster: from my mom's concerned expression to the probe moving over my stomach, from the edges of crinkly paper around my legs to the pockmarked ceiling tiles above me, from the mess of cords at the back of the computer to the baffled concern on my ultrasound tech's face. When the tech docked her probe on the ultrasound cart, she still hadn't seen what she'd been looking for.

"I think the best thing now, Riley," the tech had told us, "is for you to have an MRI. That way we can get some conclusive images about what I'm not seeing, and we can find out if it really isn't there."

For the next week or so, I tried to convince myself that those words weren't as scary as they sounded. But waiting for the MRI results had felt excruciating every day. That's why, now that I knew they were in, an afternoon of class and practice seemed endless. That's why, the minute volleyball let out, I bolted through the locker room with my gym bag at lightning speed. The whole way home, I prayed. *Please, God. Please, God.* I was already calling for my mom before I made it halfway through the back door.

She was sitting at the kitchen table, waiting. The MRI images and some documents were spread out in front of her.

"Hi," I said breathlessly, rushing to join her at the table. I took off my backpack and sat down in a single motion.

"Hey." She smiled, sort of—I couldn't quite read the expression. She sighed and squinted at me a little. "Are you ready for this?"

"Yeah."

"You sure?"

I nodded.

"Okay." She took a deep breath and exhaled.

She delivered the easy parts of the news first: that my condition was something I was born with, that it affects the center of a woman's body, and that the diagnosis explained a lot, from my dizzy spells and my bulging disk to my heart flap and every other medical puzzle I'd faced in the past few years. But my mom understood that the biggest question I had right then was the one sparked by my ultrasound: *Is it really not there?*

Without any drama or delay, Mom reached for one of the documents and one of the big images on the table. She put them both directly in front of me, pointing to five words printed at the top of the document: *Mayer-Rokitansky-Küster-Hauser syndrome.* Then she laid out the situation just as starkly as it was.

"You have this disease," she said. "It's known as MRKH, and basically what it means is that you can't have children."

I blinked. I swallowed. "Never?"

She shook her head and sighed again. "You'll never be able to."

Things in my head started to swirl. "How did the MRI tell us that?"

My mom pointed to two cloudy shapes near the left and right edges of the image.

"What this shows is that you have two ovaries, here and here, but your uterus is supposed to be right here, and it just isn't."

She paused for a time as she looked into my confused face. Then she continued.

"Your uterus is what the ultrasound tech couldn't find, and now this MRI is confirming that it's missing. This is the big marker for MRKH, unfortunately: women who have the disease are born without a uterus. So this is how we know that you have it."

One more time she let the news sink in. "I'm sorry, Ri."

For a long time I didn't say anything. Even with all the strange symptoms I'd been having, MRKH still caught me completely by surprise. I would have expected it about as much as I would have expected a fireball to fall from the sky and crash-land next to me.

*Crash*, yes. When something like this comes onto the scene, it arrives with too much force, too much speed, and too much heat to touch down smoothly. Instead, there's a collision. An explosion. A smoldering mass of debris.

I've never been the sort of person who is easily halted by much of anything, but my diagnosis stopped me cold. Even a while later, after the initial shock began to taper off, the reality of my disease still felt impossible to comprehend. I couldn't figure out how I would deal with it. I didn't have a clue how to even start trying.

# CHAPTER 23

# Unraveling

At first my thought patterns were the most frustrating part. Suddenly I had children on the brain constantly, and at the same time, it had become impossible for me to think coherently about children. Whenever kids were around and whenever kids came to mind—which was pretty much all the time now—I ended up feeling either confused, juvenile, naive, sucker punched, or some combination of all those things. I couldn't get myself to stop.

I love kids, always have. During the past four years of my life, I'd spent the vast majority of my spare time either serving children or thinking about serving children, so in that respect the thoughts weren't new. But in the past, I was always thinking about other people's kids. Now, suddenly, I'd shifted to thinking about my own.

At sixteen, on the heels of an MRKH diagnosis, I was preoccupied with thinking about "my" kids, and it felt just as bizarre as it probably should. Even though I had always assumed that one day I'd give birth to children, before my disease came into the picture, I hadn't ever given my future offspring any kind of specific thought, ever. Some teenage girls claim to already know the precise number of kids they hope to have someday. Some even go so far as to pick out enough first and middle names to cover that many children of each gender. As for me, daydreaming about kids hadn't yet been even a blip on my radar screen. I had a barely minted driver's license, and high school graduation was still more than eighteen months away. There'd be college and then maybe some grad school or a few years of a career before I'd be ready to take engagement and marriage seriously, let alone pregnancy and children. For me, any kind of future family stuff was a long way off. Now all of a sudden I had this disease. I had this nonexistent womb, and it was throwing all those other plans and ideas into upheaval.

When you haven't even begun to consider parenthood as a real possibility, the news that you can't bear children is difficult to register as a real loss. At the same time, there are opposite realities that also feel intensely true. Infertility has a way of reverberating powerfully, even for someone who has never given reproduction much thought. I would see a woman with a rounding pregnant belly and instantly think, *That will never be me.* I would catch a glimpse of kids playing on a playground and feel a little gloomy about it. I'd run across a mom with a mini-me daughter or a dad with a mini-me son, and my first thought didn't have anything to do with how cute they were together—instead, it was, *For my family, impossible.*

On the other hand, I was only sixteen. None of my classmates or peers had kids, and none of us felt like we should be having kids yet either. So, in that way there was still no *real* sense of absence for me to experience. My sense of loss wasn't an *actual* loss yet; it was just an anticipated one. I wouldn't say that I was grieving yet, but I knew with certainty that I was headed in that direction.

Is there such a thing as pre-grief? Advance sorrow? Maybe I was just trying to wrap my brain around what I'd eventually be missing, so that when the time came, I'd have some idea of how to miss it. The whole thing was a mental muddle, and some days I felt like I was unraveling. The mess of contradicting thoughts and feelings was affecting my behavior too. It was making me second-guess my reactions to things, even in circumstances that would typically seem normal. It was turning my behavior into something awkward, as if suddenly I didn't know how to conduct myself anymore. And I was making decisions in a way that seemed rash and uncharacteristic of me.

For starters, I quit the volleyball team. I did it suddenly and in the middle of the season. I have loved this sport for as long as I can remember, and I've always been a stickler for keeping my commitments. Even so, out of the blue, I told my coach that I was done. I told myself that the decision was due to group dynamics: the team vibe was getting too catty, that was all. What I failed to mention is that before the MRKH bomb went off, I had always been able to handle flare-ups in teenage friendships, no problem.

Also, I started to get weird around my boyfriend. Graham is one of the kindest, most helpful, most faithful, most dependable people I've ever met. He and I have been close friends since middle school, and we've been two peas in a pod since we started dating freshman year. (I don't know if you can legitimately use the term dating when two fourteen-year-olds are involved, but there you have it.) I had zero intentions of talking with this sixteen-year-old guy about having kids; we were nowhere near ready to get into conversations about reproduction. In addition to that, I had no reason whatsoever to think that Graham might consider ending our relationship over the status (or nonstatus) of my uterus. Nothing I had ever observed in him would give me reason to believe he would do that.

Still, a part of me was suddenly paranoid about whether MRKH could be a deal breaker for Graham someday. I started to worry that maybe, just maybe, he'd been looking for a way out of our relationship. With infertility in play, he'd have a perfectly reasonable excuse to leave. *Nobody would question that*, I told myself repeatedly. Out of nowhere, I became an insecure, crazy person in the relationship. It was embarrassing, but I couldn't figure out how to stop.

One day when Graham and I were riding in his car together, he asked me an innocent question about my recent medical appointments, and instead of responding in a way that felt honest and forthcoming, I skirted the issue.

What he said was: "Hon, are you doing okay? I mean, is there something going on for you to be having so many doctors' visits?"

His tone was concerned and sweet. Still, instantly I felt my pulse race, my stomach knot up, and my spine stiffen. "It's just some girl stuff," I told him with a shaky smile. Then I quickly changed the subject.

And one more thing: I wasn't talking with any of my friends about any of this either. I wanted to, because my friends are wonderful, and I was sure things would feel better when my girlfriends were in the loop. But I didn't feel ready yet. I worried that infertility would be a strange subject for me to bring up among teenagers. I was afraid it would be an uncomfortable issue for other people to hear about. Probably most of all, I was concerned that I'd be treated differently when news got out about my disease.

So, while typically I'd be looking to spend extra time with my close friends, I started withdrawing and isolating instead: writing in my journal, talking with my family, reading books in my room. Those are all activities I love, but doing them in part to avoid something else was making me feel lonely and sad. I felt so stuck. I understood that things would never go back to the way they were before my diagnosis, and I understood that big changes are extremely hard to absorb. I tried to be patient with myself and wait out the process of coming to terms with my new reality, but I couldn't help feeling anxious, like it wasn't happening nearly fast enough.

What I wanted was for all this newness to start feeling normal. What I wanted was to begin picking up the pieces somehow so I could move on. What I wanted was a little forward progress. Yet on top of *not* sorting through my thoughts and *not* straightening out my behavior, forward progress seemed to be another big *not* for me as well. All I seemed able to do was look backward. I was giving no real consideration to the future and whatever events might be coming down the road. Instead, over and over I rehashed things that had already happened.

Why was I doing it? I was finding that with each chapter I reopened, I was reassessing what that chapter should mean and how much significance it should hold now. It was as if my past view on my life didn't pan out and was in need of revision. It was as if I were looking for a whole new perspective, because maybe with a different angle I'd feel like I could make sense of my life again. All of these old chapters had had a clear, coherent purpose; they wove together seamlessly, part of a story I understood. Now suddenly the whole tapestry was unraveling, and in the middle of the chaos, I had a strong suspicion: all of this had something to do with Kenya.

# CHAPTER 24

# A Hope and a
## *Future*

A few weeks after my MRKH diagnosis, I got up the nerve to tell my friend Kassadee what was going on. I'd been isolating and withdrawing long enough, and I decided it was time to open up. After all, if anybody could help me figure out how to move forward with this thing, my best friend ranked at the top of the list.

Kassadee and I have been close since we were in elementary school. We were both in the same smallish school district growing up, where we connected over a shared love for the same kinds of books. We would swap recommendations and imagine ourselves as our favorite characters together, convinced we were just like them. It was the perfect friendship glue for two avid readers, and our book conversations are still part of what keeps us so close.

Over the years, Kassadee and I have gotten to know pretty much everything there is for two young women to know about each other. We don't hold back on sharing details, even when they're tough. In many ways, Kassadee has modeled that for me. Her mom has a rare disease of unknown cause that includes chronic pain. It's a hard, ongoing struggle that affects their whole family. While I wish that the reality for Kassadee and her family was different, at the same time, I have been privileged to watch them all deal with the harsh realities of chronic illness with grace. I have seen the strength of their faith put on display as they trust God in the midst of questions and suffering. That was already inspiring to me, long before my MRKH made it something I could relate to personally.

So, as I looked ahead to a conversation with my best friend, I knew already that she'd have helpful things to say. I expected that her perspective would probably shed some light on things. And I hoped that she'd help me get to a point where I could trust God firmly again rather than spiritually swinging in the wind.

On the day of our meeting, I got to the coffee shop a little early, with time enough to claim a quiet booth in the corner. Kassadee arrived a few minutes after me. After ordering our drinks, we sat down, took one sip each, and looked at each other. For a few seconds, we both waited. Then I took a deep breath and the telling began.

I took a page out of my mom's playbook and said the hardest thing first. "My doctors found out that I have this disease called MRKH, and it means I can't ever have kids." Kassadee's initial nonverbal response was so kind and concerned that it opened the floodgates. For the next two hours, we talked about everything.

Well, at first mostly I talked and Kassadee listened. I explained how one doctor's appointment kept leading to another and another until my diagnosis was in. Then she listened some more while I started processing things out loud, going into detail about how confused, lost, and frustrated I was.

"I just don't understand why God would let this happen to me," I told her. "You know how much I love kids, and I know I'd be a good mom, so why this? I see teenagers getting pregnant before they're married, but I'm trying to obey God's plan and I end up never being able to have kids? What did I do wrong? I mean, after all the ways I've tried to follow God and serve him, do I really deserve *this*?"

Kassadee listened patiently. I released a big sigh and continued, telling her I'd been digging into God's Word almost insatiably, looking for an answer or some solace or a little help or just *something*. I told her I was spending hours in prayer and had filled pages and pages in my journal. I told her it didn't seem like it was helping.

"I *know* hard things happen to everybody," I said. "And I *get* that being a Christian doesn't mean life will be easy. The thing is—I guess I just really, really don't understand."

With that I stopped talking.

Kassadee took a couple of sips of her hot chocolate, letting everything sink in. Then she put down her mug and leaned toward me over the table.

"Riley," she said, "those thoughts and questions make perfect sense. I can see why you would be thinking all of that." (I told you Kassadee knew how to be a good friend.)

For the next few minutes, Kassadee recounted some of the ways that she and her family had interrogated God over the years, wanting answers different from the ones they were getting. She acknowledged how hard it is to handle disappointment, especially when there is no reason to expect it will go away. And she told me she wanted to be an encouragement and support to me, however I need her to be.

"You know, Riley, I just keep thinking about Jeremiah 29:11: 'For I know the plans I have for you . . . plans to prosper you and not to harm you, plans to give you hope and a future.' I keep thinking that when you were thirteen, you went all the way to the other side of the world and fell in love. God brought you to a place where there are so many orphans—so many kids without moms—and now here you are, not able to have children of your own."

She stopped for a few seconds, as if she wasn't sure whether she should continue. She bit her bottom lip for a moment, then shrugged slightly. "Maybe all this is happening because God is telling you something about your future. Maybe he called you to Kenya because it's an opportunity to care for more kids than you could ever have yourself."

There in the coffee shop, in the moment when she brought up the orphans and Kenya, it was just a whiff of an idea to me. Everything else from our conversation still felt too raw, and I was nowhere near ready to digest a new perspective. But in the days and weeks that followed, I kept hearing Kassadee's words over and over in my head, and I started to experience them like a long, low rumble—like a quake going right down the center of me. And for the first time in a while, I started to think about the future.

# CHAPTER 25

# A New
## *Direction*

Was Kenya supposed to continue to be a big part of my life? Was serving East African orphans the ministry I was being called to? Was Kassadee onto something, seeing a trajectory I wasn't yet seeing, when she suggested that to me?

Or was it possible instead that those options were just mental detours around my grief? Could it be that I was considering them because I wanted my MRKH to have "purpose" and meaning? Was I just looking for something good to come out of my diagnosis, or was God really at work here? And if he *was* at work, then what did that mean?

Discovering my MRKH precisely when I needed to start thinking about my long-term future was no coincidence. In the years before then, I had been to so many doctors' appointments, had been given so many tests, and had been asked by my mom so often whether something was wrong, my diagnosis could have been discovered years before. Instead, it came to light when it did. My work in Kenya came sharply into focus because it was a deeply important part of my life, and because in a crisis, priorities put themselves in order easily. After having worried about myself and my own future for weeks, suddenly those personal issues were being trumped by something more important.

Over time I saw that it wasn't some kind of cruel irony that a girl who loves kids ended up with a disease that will forever keep her from having her own. As painful and disappointing as my diagnosis was (and still is), it also became, amazingly, a source of solace and even joy. I started to see that if MRKH made me more dependent on God and more interested in serving others, then MRKH could be not just a useful thing but a *good* thing in my life. Maybe one day I would even be able to look back and say I would have chosen it if given the chance.

So as my senior year approached, on top of looking at college options and thinking ahead to graduation, I began praying about what, exactly, God was pointing me toward in Kenya. How would a focus on orphans be different from the work that Generation Next had done already? Did continued service in Kenya mean sticking with a one-trip-per-year rhythm as I'd been doing up till now, or would it require something more?

As I was doing all this praying, one idea came to mind repeatedly: Generation Next could fund and operate an orphanage. We could do it in the community where we had been working for the past three years, where we had strong relationships with people we trusted. We would have no problem hiring good workers, and through our contacts in Kenya, we could even keep an eye on the place when we were back home in the United States.

I won't go so far as to say that running an orphanage seemed like an easy thing to take on, especially considering all the red tape wrapped around Robin's efforts, which had so far prevented her from starting a children's home at Namba House. Still, I was optimistic. I'd come across other orphanages doing excellent work in Kenya, so why couldn't we?

With the help of my parents and my contacts in Kenya, I

started to look into the possibility of purchasing property or buy-ing a building. This was far beyond anything Generation Next had considered so far, but I had faith that God could open doors and provide funds, just as he had so many times before.

I waded into the international legalese, looking to figure out what paperwork would be required and what kind of process would need to be followed. And I looked into staffing and operational needs, working to understand how much money and how many local workers we would need to get an orphanage up and running and then to keep it going. I also contacted several friends who help run orphanages in Africa, all in different places. Since they had managed to do the very thing I was considering, and since they each did it in a slightly different way, I assumed they would be a wealth of information, resources, and ideas.

They weren't. To a person, each of my orphanage-running friends told me that the process is much more difficult than it might seem. They told me horror stories about property acquisi-tion, orphanage permits, and legal fees. They told me it could take a decade to get everything approved. My friend in South Africa was particularly blunt: "Absolutely do not do it."

I took their thoughts and advice to heart. By the same token, however, I also reminded myself that God had exceeded expecta-tions multiple times during my experiences in Africa. So I prayed for wisdom and understanding. I asked God to reveal what a long-term commitment to orphans in Kenya might mean. Then I waited to see which doors he would open and which ones he would close.

# CHAPTER 26

# OUT OF THE
## *Blue*

A little more than a month after my MRKH diagnosis, we got not one, but two, significant, unexpected offers from people in Kenya. Put together, they made long-term service in Africa suddenly seem more possible while answering the orphan question too.

The first out-of-the-blue request came from Robin. My parents and I received an email from her, telling us that she'd like to discuss something important. Would we be able to chat with her sometime in the next few days?

We set something up right away. We were excited to hear what Robin had to say, especially following my conversation with Kassadee. I'd begun to think about Kibwezi in a new way, wondering whether God might be calling me to live there permanently someday. Had God brought me to Bomet, then to Kibwezi, on a journey from pencils and a hospital to maxi pads and a school, all because he had an even bigger adventure in store?

When Robin popped up on our computer screen, we spent a few minutes catching up, then Robin got right to it.

"You're probably wondering why I asked to video chat and why I asked to do it with all three of you."

We all smiled and nodded.

"Well, as you know, we've been trying to get clearance for the children's home at Namba House. It hasn't come together yet, and I'm starting to wonder if that's the right direction for Namba to go in Kibwezi right now. The reason why I'm reaching out to you is that the building is bigger than we need right now and bigger than we expect we'll ever need. We can still use it for some of our projects, but I'm wondering if Generation Next might have use for the rest of the building. Would you?"

My parents and I were mute for a moment, just staring at the screen. Then Mom and Dad both turned to me and waited while I tried to find some words.

I told Robin how kind her offer was and asked her if we would be renting from her.

"The short answer is no," she said. "We constructed the building at an affordable cost, and I'm not interested in being a landlord. What I'm proposing to you is that if you're willing to fix up your part of the building, then I would let you use it for the foreseeable future for free. It's in good shape already, but, you know, get the furnishings and paint that you'd need . . ."

Another awed silence. Dad, Mom, and I eventually got our vocal chords working enough to ask some additional questions. Then we asked Robin if we could take a few weeks to think about her offer, and she said she understood.

Toward the end of our chat, I was already thinking that it probably wouldn't work out. Although nearly everything about the possibility sounded amazing, it also seemed premature. While Generation Next had been strongly considering starting an orphanage in Kibwezi, if we wanted to do that, it was going to require a lot more time and money than we were used to investing. Maybe in a couple of years an offer like Robin's might work for us, but at this point it seemed like we would be biting off far more than we could chew.

After talking with Robin, we spent two weeks trying to figure out a way that we could make it work. We crunched numbers, but we couldn't figure out a single realistic strategy. There's having faith, and then there's crazy. Without the resources to back up such a significant project, the idea was beyond wild.

Then one morning my mom got an unexpected call from a local woman named Marilyn. My family had heard of Marilyn from some friends of ours, but none of us had ever spoken with her. She and her husband run the Branson Boys and Girls Club, and as part of their work with the organization, they operated a thrift shop downtown. The storefront was an ongoing source of revenue for their nonprofit, but they were looking to get out of thrifting.

Marilyn offered Generation Next the store. As simple as that. We could have it all, she said—the inventory, the building, everything. The place was fully functional, with a couple thousand square feet of fully stocked retail space on top of several storage rooms and a loading dock. It was expected to generate tens of thousands of dollars of income in a year. We would have a lot of work on our hands, but Generation Next would generate a consistent cash flow for the first time ever. If we wanted the shop, it was ours!

Within just a few weeks, Mom and Dad helped me take over the books for the shop, and we all started volunteering at Riley's Treasures downtown. Once again we were seeing God's wild side in all its glory, and Generation Next's orphanage was no longer just a dream.

# CHAPTER 27

# WALKING ON
## *Water*

It didn't take long in the life of Riley's Treasures for it to become a staging ground for our next trip to Kenya. This trip was going to be unlike any that Generation Next had sponsored before, and we expected that it would be the start of something that would continue in Kibwezi for a long, long time.

Part of our plan involved filling an entire shipping container full of orphanage supplies and organizing our largest group of volunteers ever, twenty-one people. We began to set aside clothes, shoes, cribs, beds, baby gear—whatever we might need to help care for orphans in Kenya. Despite the warnings from my international friends, it seemed clear that God was opening the doors necessary for Generation Next to make an orphanage happen.

Trying to start an international orphanage in a matter of months was quite a goal, but it seemed to be going off without a hitch. People in Branson were donating to the cause in droves, dropping off diapers, onesies, kids' socks and underwear, books, furniture, pretty much whatever they thought we might need. We kept stowing it away, getting more and more excited about our orphanage as the piles grew. Churches and local businesses were once again stepping up to help in big ways, this time by covering a large chunk of our container's shipping fees.

My family and I were crazy busy. My parents had two high school students and a middle schooler. We were suddenly the owners of a thrift shop, not to mention the rooms and rooms of goods inside it. We were about to open an orphanage in Kenya, involving another international trip and all the logistics that would entail. And we were trying to keep up with regular parts of life too: church, school, sporting events, friendships—the whole gamut.

Along with all that, I'd been chosen to participate in another trip as well. Every year, a family in Arkansas hosts a small group of American high school seniors on a visit to Israel. They fund a ten-day exploration of the Holy Land, where students tour well-known locations from Scripture and experience them firsthand. A pastor travels with the group, teaching biblical history lessons at every stop along the way. The goal of the trip is to prepare students to better share God's story wherever life after high school may lead.

When I heard about the Israel trip, I was thrilled about potentially having the chance to increase my Bible knowledge and understanding. Many of my friends in Kenya would most likely never have reason to travel out of their own villages, much less their own country. On their own they wouldn't get to see the setting and geography of Scripture come alive. But someone else could go and then bring the stories to them. The whole time leading up to the trip, I got giddy just thinking about it!

When spring break came, the group of selected students gathered in New York and then flew together to Israel. We saw things that I'd been reading about in Scripture my whole life: the Jordan River, the Western Wall, the Garden Tomb. We climbed Masada, one of Herod's fortresses, and discussed the zealots who chose death there over slavery in Rome. Every location was a lesson, and it felt like I was learning more than ever before.

But learning wasn't the only thing I did on the trip. Part of the goal was that students would be equipped to share what they were learning about God, so each of us was asked to give a part of our testimony at some point during the trip. As it turned out, my time came in the middle of the Sea of Galilee.

Our pastor had just reminded us all that it was on this very sea in Jesus' time that a storm churned up and, in the midst of it, Jesus was seen calmly walking on the water. Jesus' disciples were in a boat afraid when they saw him, but Jesus called out to one of them, Peter, beckoning him to join him on the waves.

Amazingly, Peter got out of the boat and for a while was walking to Jesus on top of the sea. But then Peter noticed the wind, became frightened, and began sinking. Jesus helped him back up, chided him for doubting, and brought him back safely to the boat. At that point the wind stopped, and the disciples worshiped Jesus, proclaiming him to be the Son of God.

As I sat in a boat, listening to a story about Jesus and doubt, I couldn't help but think it was a fitting time for me to share my testimony. I looked out over that big lake and tried to picture the kind of terrifying storm that we were told can still whip up over the Sea of Galilee. I tried to picture Jesus walking on the water, wondering if I would have enough faith to walk out to him. Even though I knew he has promised that he won't give me anything more than I can handle, I still wasn't sure I would trust him to keep me above the waves when my next storm came. I hoped so. After all, he had proven himself more than faithful, even in the aftermath of my diagnosis of MRKH.

That's essentially what I shared with the other students and the chaperones that day out on the sea. As our little boat bobbed up and down on top of gentle waves, I told them about my MRKH and how I first reacted to it. "I stepped out into Kenya, ready to trust God with whatever he was going to use me for," I said. "But as soon as something rough hit me, I lost sight of the most important person standing in front of me, and instead I tried to think about how I could control the situation. As soon as I did that, I began to drown. I was thrashing about until Jesus took hold of me and settled me down, helping me to see some purpose in what he was doing."

I had a difficult time getting through sharing that. It was so personal to me and still pretty painful. But as I told the group about what God had done in my life since (and because of) my diagnosis, I started to feel my own internal storm calming a little more than it had so far. I looked out over the water and thanked God for the ways he had rescued me from myself and my doubts. I thought about how I wanted to keep my eyes on him better in the future rather than get overwhelmed by the wind.

We still had a few months before our fifth trip to Kenya. Little did I know it, but there were more Sea of Galilee moments just ahead.

# CHAPTER 28

# SHATTERED
# *Dreams*

Six weeks before our 2014 trip, two explosions went off in Mombasa. At the beach, a man had dropped his backpack in the sand and walked away as if to swim, and soon after that a homemade bomb in the bag went off.[1] Thankfully, everyone in the area survived, but in town a live hand grenade was tossed into a group of travelers at a busy bus terminal, killing three people.

Early news reports suggested that the attacks were coordinated and carried out by militant Islamist extremists from neighboring Somalia. Countries all over the world responded by issuing official advisories for those traveling to Kenya. Hundreds of European tourists on the coast were evacuated almost immediately.[2] Five of the people who had planned to participate in our trip decided to cancel.

A completely natural response for the rest of us would have been to run for the hills as well. Never wanting to go back would have been perfectly understandable, having glimpsed the potential dangers and the widespread corruption that exist there. For plenty of people I know, the day-to-day risks in Kenya have made it a place they would never consider traveling to in the first place. And the concerns people have make sense to me. I recognize them because

I've had them myself plenty of times. Thinking we could travel around Kenya (or any country, for that matter) risk-free would be ignorant and foolish, and it's for that reason that our Generation Next groups take great care to be diligent about safety while we're in the country. We know the risks are real, and we understand that they really could impact us. That said, the troubles in the region have never kept us away from Kenya. In fact, you could argue that those troubles have been a deciding factor in what keeps calling us back.

We contacted a missionary family living in Nairobi to ask for their input, and they assured us that while the city was probably less secure than Branson, no imminent danger was known. We could expect Kibwezi to be unaffected, they told us. So our group of sixteen Americans decided to fly as planned.

But there was one hiccup. Two weeks before the start of our trip, our container of orphanage supplies was due to arrive in Kibwezi, and it didn't show. We did some calling and emailing about it, only to find out that it was stuck in customs somewhere. "How long will it stay there?" we asked several different sources. "No telling," was the response. *Was someone looking to bribe us?* we wondered. Probably.

We emailed and called Kenyan Immigration every day, trying to get the container moving. Nothing changed. We contacted everyone we could think of who might be able to motivate someone involved in the process, and none of it did any good. We started to worry a little. Aside from the walls, the floor, the roof, and the people, our entire orphanage was in that crate, and it wasn't budging. The longer it took, the bigger the problem, especially because we had planned our trip in two stages.

All sixteen of us would be there for three weeks getting the orphanage ready and delivering school supplies. At the three-week mark, everybody except Mom and I and Graham and Rachel,

Graham's younger sister, would go home, and then the four of us would stay in Kibwezi for one more month to finalize legal details. If the container didn't arrive within the first two weeks or so of our trip, we would be stuck trying to do everything ourselves, and we didn't see how that would be possible. We prayed fervently. We asked others to pray. We prayed some more. Finally, we left for Kenya, knowing our container still hadn't arrived.

After two days in transit, we arrived in Nairobi well past sunset. We spent our first few hours in a hotel to avoid traveling in the dark and left the city at first light. Before we went, my mom sent a few more emails about our container, hoping we would have a response by the time we arrived in Kibwezi.

Our rented bus took us straight to Namba House, which would be home to our whole group for the duration of the trip and house Mom, Graham, Rachel, and I for an additional month. After a day of rest to reset our internal clocks and get settled, fourteen of our team members began cleaning cobwebs and wasps' nests out of the ceilings and adding a fresh coat of paint to some walls in the house. Meanwhile, Mom and I went to see about potential employees for the orphanage. We had prearranged several meetings with applicants already, most of whom we knew from Kambua and elsewhere in town. Each of them was going to meet us at Namba House one at a time so we could hear from them and they could get a sense of the place all in one fell swoop.

Our first few interviews for orphanage employees took place that afternoon. We were looking for women to oversee the home and care for the children year-round. Since whoever we hired would be living on property that still belonged to Namba, Robin had asked to be part of the interviews, and we had agreed to it.

Mom and I had prepared a long list of questions for our applicants, mostly centering on who they were individually, how they cared for children, and what they believed about God and faith.

The first two women we interviewed were both Christians, and as we went through the list with them, it seemed clear that Robin was getting a little uncomfortable during the God and faith questions. We knew that she was not a believer, but we were a little surprised that our line of questioning seemed to be a problem for her.

Then we began interviewing a man who shared over the course of the meeting that he was Muslim. We explained to him that the orphanage would be an explicitly Christian home, and unfortunately, we wouldn't be hiring anyone who didn't share at least the fundamentals of our Christian faith. As we said this, I saw Robin begin to fume.

Mom and I stood to thank the interviewee for his time. Robin, on the other hand, didn't even speak. She nodded to the man and then stood rigidly in the corner, a clear ball of nerves. I ushered the man to the door and made sure he got through the gate okay, then walked back toward our interview room. I wasn't even halfway there before I could hear Robin's voice.

"I don't want that kind of thing happening in my building." She spoke calmly but forcefully. I could tell she was outraged.

Mom had a confused look on her face. "What kind of thing are you talking about?" my mom asked her.

"You just rejected that man because he's a Muslim."

"Robin," she said evenly, "you know we're Christians, and you know that's the primary reason why we're in Kibwezi at all. What kind of orphanage did you think we were going to be running?"

"I'm totally against that kind of discrimination, and I won't stand for it."

Here I cut in. "But we're going to expect the workers here to tell the kids about God and Jesus. That's a huge part of their job description. If they don't follow Jesus like we do, it's going to be impossible for them to share about him."

"That's not important to me," Robin replied tersely. "I don't want this to happen again." Then she stormed out.

Later that evening I wrote in my journal, "It will work out. It has to work out." There was a giant shipping container full of furnishings and supplies on its way, and Namba House was the only building at our disposal. We had been working up to this for a year—surely God wouldn't grind our efforts to a halt now. Plus, this was the thing that helped make sense out of my MRKH—certainly he wouldn't let all my questions come roaring back again. Would he shatter our dreams for an orphanage, just like that?

The next day, Mom, Robin, and I interviewed several more candidates for the orphanage positions. This time around, the God-focused questions didn't get tense; in fact, between interviews, when we took a few minutes to review the applicants' qualifications, Robin offered no opinions on any of them.

When we were finished with the interviews, I told Robin I wanted to talk some more about this being a Christian home and what that meant.

"You know," she said, "I've decided that if this works out, you can do what you want about that. But before I file paperwork to get an orphanage approved here, I just want to make sure that what we're doing is the best fit for everyone involved. It needs to work really well for me, it needs to work well for you, it needs to work well for Planned Parenthood . . ." With that last bit she trailed off, but she was looking at us pointedly.

"Planned Parenthood?" my mom questioned.

"Yeah, I'm going to ask them to share part of our space too. I think the services they offer are really needed around here."

"Robin," I said, "Planned Parenthood does abortions."

"Well, yeah, and birth control. Birth control would be the main thing."

*"Robin."* My mom this time. "We can't share a door and a gate and a roof with an abortion clinic."

"Why not?" Her voice was nonchalant, but there was just enough ice in her eyes to let us know that her intent wasn't.

My shoulders sagged and my back slumped. Suddenly I felt so defeated. I began piling my interview notes into one stack, shaking my head and trying to breathe evenly.

"Okay," I said. "If you're sure that's what you're going to do, then we're going to have to leave. We're not going to be able to do our work at Namba House. We're looking to save kids in Kibwezi. We're not going to partner with a place that's okay with killing them."

We were only two days into our biggest project ever, and suddenly it was over.

# CHAPTER 29

# BITTERSWEET
## *Deliveries*

While waiting for our container to arrive, we reordered our plan. The days we were going to spend sprucing up Namba House and preparing the orphanage, we spent doing other projects. Namba House is so big that there is always plenty of cleaning and fixing up to be done.

When our container finally arrived, the semi driver backed it inside the Namba property's gate and climbed down from his cab. After opening a couple of big latches and taking a hacksaw to the lock on the back, he swung the door open and we got to work. We didn't know what in the world we were going to do with all our supplies now, but we couldn't leave them in the crate. All the cribs and dressers, all the stuffed animals, all the totes of school supplies, all the deflated soccer balls, all the boxes of baby clothes—everything was there. We moved it all into the house using a bucket brigade line, and even the local kids helped to heft things off the truck. By early afternoon, the main room at Namba House was nothing but piles and piles of boxes.

I had been praying that Robin would change her mind about the tenants in the building. But each day, as our date of departure drew nearer, despite insisting in my journal over and over that "It's

UNLOADING THE CONTAINER WE SHIPPED

going to work out, it's going to work out," eventually I had to start dealing with reality: maybe it wouldn't.

Mom, Graham, and I met one night to talk about our options. I was feeling discouraged and angry. Most of our school supplies had already been distributed, and we still had a room full of orphanage supplies to deal with. Robin didn't have use for them, and they couldn't just stay where they were, clogging up the center of the building. There is no such thing as a storage unit in Kibwezi either. We had one option, as far as any of us could tell: we had to get rid of everything. The question was how.

We decided we would make up "new-mother kits" that could be given out to women who'd just given birth at local hospitals. Since moms didn't typically stay in the hospital more than a day after delivery, we could make rounds every day to a whole new group of women, passing out clothes, baby bathtubs, and more. That would help us get rid of some of the smaller items we had brought with us. For the bigger items like cribs and dressers, we consulted with a local pastor who knew the community and provided us with a short list of families who could use the furniture.

So it was settled. The next morning we started sifting through boxes, making boy kits and girl kits for moms at nearby hospitals. As I put together a stack of baby boys' onesies in various sizes, knowing a needy kid in Kibwezi would get to grow into them, I couldn't help but feel happy about that. But at the same time, I was thinking that these clothes wouldn't be worn by a little boy at our orphanage, and that thought made me heartsick.

The delivery process was similarly bittersweet—joy and mourning mingling together. With every new-mother kit we distributed, I was painfully aware that our plan for the orphanage had just died a little more. At the same time, it was like we were having several mini baby showers every day, and it would be pretty hard to be upset about that!

The three-week mark in the trip came, and just Mom, Graham, Rachel, and I were left in the upstairs apartment by ourselves. The place felt beyond desolate, with everyone else gone and all the container supplies passed out. It was too much quiet and too much empty space for just us and our troubles.

With Namba House off the table, we began to scout local real estate. Someday we were going to need a building, and that meant we either needed to purchase an existing structure, or we needed to buy land and build. There are hardly any buildings on the market in Kibwezi, and of the ones that are, we wouldn't want to buy any of them. All the places that could be big enough are businesses, so they're not set up properly for home life. It would take significant renovation just to make a place marginally useful.

So we were left with the option to build, but the idea of starting from empty ground, getting all the permits required, and going through every construction hurdle felt exhausting. All we could think was that it would take forever, and we would be asked to pay bribes left and right. On one recent drive to Nairobi, we had been stopped twice by two different police officers within a span of about five kilometers. The stated reason for both stops was that we had "too many people in the backseat," which was true. But one look around revealed that *most* of the cars on the road that day had too many people in the backseat. The only difference between those cars and ours was that our too-many-people were white.

"Just imagine," I said to Mom, "trying to buy land, get materials, and pay builders for as long as it takes to finish a whole orphanage."

"And how many times people would try to shake us down for more money," Mom said. "How much extra would we end up paying? How much longer would we have to wait?"

We were spinning our wheels and not getting anywhere. What had started out as frustration and confusion had quickly turned into cynicism. Some days we felt nearly hopeless. We kept praying for God to provide, but at the end of every day, we came up empty.

Then one morning, with a little more than a month left of our time in Kibwezi, as usual we woke up to an email from my dad. We expected to open it and find his typical encouragement, positivity, and insight. Instead, we found something more fitting to the reality we were dealing with.

> *Tracy and Riley,*
>
> *I changed your flights—I hope you don't mind. Your new itineraries are attached. I think it's time for you to come home.*
>
> *Love you both.*

He was right. Mom and I both knew it instantly. We opened our new itineraries and found that we had just a week left in Kenya. We arranged for a ride to the airport. We started saying good-bye to our friends for another year. We packed our things.

The morning of our departure, our friend Silas picked us up with a car and driver, and we loaded in. As we drove away I looked back at the building we had planned to fill with children, heartsick that it stood nearly empty. I still wasn't sure what to think about that. We had come here this year expecting to start making Kenya my home. Everything was going to feel right at last. The storm that had started with MRKH would finally feel like it was settling a little. But instead, the whole thing churned up again, maybe bigger than ever, and now all I wanted to do was leave.

During the weeks ahead, as I reflected on all the ups and downs I'd experienced in Kenya and at home, I had to concede that the truth about following Jesus is that sometimes it involves taking roads that don't seem to lead anywhere that's good. Sometimes there is only one hairpin turn after another. Sometimes all we can see are potholes ahead and a likelihood that we'll end up stranded.

For a while our core Generation Next group tried to figure out where we went wrong. What warnings did we miss? Should we have canceled the delivery of the shipping container? Had we been rash in agreeing to accept Robin's out-of-the-blue offer? Was it foolish to attempt to open an international orphanage? Should we have taken things more slowly from the start? Could we have done more research first? Should we reconsider the whole idea, and maybe nix my plan to live in Kenya long term?

They were all questions worth mulling over, and we would give them serious consideration. But we would have been missing the point, I think, if we focused only on them. I believe that God was reminding us that even when following Jesus leads us into a storm, he is the calm in the storm. Sometimes he still asks us to venture out on the water, in the pitch-black night, in the middle of the raging squall, and at times he lets us feel like we're sinking and about to drown. But every storm that makes us look to and call out for him is a good thing. Our group reminded each other that our hope and strength would come from God's presence alone, and that was plenty enough reason to praise.

We ended up deciding that an orphanage was too ambitious a starting point. We would begin with foster care instead, or maybe a community center with sewing classes and meals for some of the villagers a couple of times a week. We would find some land and build on it, and it would take a while. There was no rush to figure it all out immediately; we were willing to wait until things came together.

In the meantime we would keep watching the real estate market in Kibwezi, and we would keep returning in the summers, doing what we had come to know best there. We would get a group together and round up thousands of school supplies. We would make hygiene kits galore. We would string beads onto bracelets that proclaim God's story of redemption. That was the sum total of the plan—at least until Robin called.

She got my parents and me on the phone together again and proceeded to tell us that she'd reconsidered. She explained to us that she'd given the whole situation careful thought over the past few months and decided that as she aged, she'd started to feel less and less up to running everything with Namba. In particular she would soon be looking to sell her charity's property in Kibwezi. If we were interested in buying and could make arrangements to do so, she said, Namba House could be ours.

We were astonished! Just like that, our plans could flip-flop! This was just a *potential* plan now, though, because we were committed to not getting ahead of ourselves. But as we started to consider it, the idea only seemed to get better and better. With the apartment upstairs, Namba House would certainly work as a home. It was big enough to house some foster children *and* a community center. The solar power, crops, and ponds would help it be self-sustaining. And, thanks to the change of plans the previous summer, the place had just received a really good scrub and a fresh coat of paint. Not to mention, with the building already standing, we wouldn't have to wait for construction or for land. If everything worked out, we could move forward soon!

I really tried not to get my hopes up. I was surprised that Robin was making an offer so soon after our disagreement. But God is faithful and always present. Even though Robin claims not to be a believer, I think God was continually working on her heart through her relationship with us. She knew we only meant well in our intentions for using Namba House, but I think maybe she worried that it would be a struggle to work with followers of Christ. Religion can be an intimidating thing, especially when you don't share the same opinions and perspectives. But perhaps as Robin saw that our primary goal was simply to be faithful in following Christ, she realized we weren't going to get all caught up in a "my religion is better than yours" power struggle.

I serve an amazing God who is always surprising me. He is always a step ahead. He knew how things would go with Robin, and it was part of his design. As we stepped back and carefully considered our overall goals in Kenya, instead of focusing on one particular thing, God revealed his plan at the perfect time, just as he always does. All I can do is smile and say, "You got me again."

# CHAPTER 30

# PLANTING THE
## *Future*

A nother summer came, and Generation Next returned to Kibwezi. For the first time ever, my brothers came along with me and Mom and Dad, and the five of us made up more than a third of our team of twelve. We stayed at Kambua Guest House, where some recent construction had stirred up a lot of scorpions. We had to dodge them constantly!

I couldn't wait to show my brothers everything that had become so dear to me. Soon after we arrived, my family made the rounds—me grinning from ear to ear.

The tilapia ponds at Namba House had been extended, the crops had gone through another cycle, and bananas were growing everywhere. One bunch was even ripening in the chicken coop!

Pamoja was in the process of getting another classroom, an extension off one end of the existing one. Yes, our school was doing so well that it was ready to take on another whole group of kids! The original Pamoja kids were two years older than they were when we met them, and they were thriving in their studies. Because they had been provided with meals every school day, they were not only taller, but their bellies were fuller too.

Eunice and John introduced us to their new baby, their third boy. Eunice straps him to her back while teaching at Pamoja, the cutest educational tool ever.

Mumo, having always had a closely shaved head of hair, was now sporting two-inch dreadlocks. When he speaks proudly about owning his own shop that sells SIM cards and cell phones, he sounds like Kibwezi's businessman of the year! He is committed to helping out Generation Next whenever he can.

I was overjoyed when we caught up with Barbara. She had graduated secondary school and was planning to expand her first-hand knowledge of the world. She had applied to university in the States—in Branson, Missouri, of all places! Her scores on a required international entrance test were good, and she was expecting to start college in the fall. She was already joking about meeting an American husband. I knew that her dad, Burgwin, would be around to help get us where we need to go in Kibwezi or make connections with schools we wished to visit.

We completed the sale of Namba House in January 2016 and have already been making improvements on the building and will continue renovating a little at a time. We'll also continue to deliver school supplies and pass out hygiene kits. We'll visit kids in hospitals and orphanages, putting God's love on display one piece of hard candy at a time. Everywhere we go, we'll keep dreaming about the future of this place we've come to love so much. With each trip we'll attempt to do more work than ever before, both a bigger volume and a broader scope, working furiously.

From the beginning I think we shouldered it all because we felt compelled to. If *we* didn't bring supplies, how many kids would have to go without? If *we* didn't finish the school, who would? If *we* didn't care about the need for hygiene items, which teen girls would turn to prostitution? If *we* didn't help out at the clinic, what financial hardships would local families have to endure? And if *we* didn't start an orphanage, where were the orphans in Kibwezi to go?

Such thinking is not necessarily a bad thing. But it's not necessarily all good either. In the middle of trying to do everything, sometimes you lose sight of who is really in charge, and you start believing that you need to do everything—which, of course, no teenager can and no nonprofit can either.

Often after events where I've shared about Generation Next, I've had conversations with people who are looking for ways to serve. That's one of my favorite subjects to chat about, and I love hearing how God is directing people to give to others. I can't tell you how many times I've met someone who has said something like, "I could deliver school supplies in Kenya!" or "I could collect hygiene products and make kits!"

While I don't doubt that they could, and maybe better than Generation Next can, the question I always pose to them is not about *could* but *called*. God doesn't lead everybody into medical mission work, even though it is vital to the health of many people in countries around the world. And God doesn't lead everybody into full-time evangelism either, even though that's a definite need as well. No, he calls some people to spearhead microfinance initiatives. He calls others to learn languages and translate Bibles. And sometimes he writes backpacks and maxi pads onto his servants' hearts.

If I've learned anything about calling over the course of my years serving in Kenya, it's this: you can do something because it's possible, and you can do something because you can't *not* do it. There is a striking difference between the two. We signed on to the medical clinic with Namba because it was an opportunity that was made available to us, because it met an important need at the time. It was a good cause, so we thought it would be good for us to contribute to. The school stuff and the hygiene kits, on the other hand, were things we couldn't *not* do.

When you're serving just because you *can*, the work is useful and beneficial and good. But you'll stay committed to it only as

BEST SUPPORT TEAM EVER!! CAMERON BANKS, GRAHAM SNYDER, ME, JACOB BANKS, LUCAS BANKS, TRACY BANKS. PICTURE TAKEN AT THE KEETER CENTER ON THE CAMPUS OF COLLEGE OF THE OZARKS.

long as it stays convenient. By contrast, when you're serving in a capacity where you feel *called*, you'll move heaven and earth if you have to, to see it through.

During the rest of our trip, the twelve of us hosted a vacation Bible school and delivered school supplies and hygiene kits. Before heading home, we took time out to plant some trees together. This is becoming a tradition all over Kenya, part of an effort to rebuild some of the greenery lost because of recent drought conditions. My planting partner was Graham. He was on his fourth trip to Kibwezi, so he and I had both been growing roots here for a long time.

I didn't know it yet, but a couple of months later, Graham would kneel before me on a Branson riverbank and propose with my grandmother's wedding ring. The following year we would be deep into our wedding planning and looking forward to sharing the rest of our lives.

On our next trip to Kenya we'll be working on the community center we purchased, and we'll have a traditional Kenyan wedding with our Kenyan family. After Graham finishes school, we'll plan our move to Namba House, our future home. We can't wait to live with and serve the people of Kibwezi, surrounded by the sounds of children.

# Acknowledgments

## FROM RILEY

A special thank-you to Dad and Mom for never once thinking that my dreams were too big. For instilling in each of their children a desire to work hard and to never give up. Our faith and family are the most important things we have. To Jacob and Cameron, my awesome brothers, for sacrificing their time and weekends, not to mention always helping and traveling with us. I love you all very much!

Graham, I can't thank you enough for letting me follow my calling and never leaving my side. We have tackled some things that neither of us would have expected we'd have to deal with. I am grateful for your kind heart and your love for the Lord. When I told you that I had been diagnosed with MRKH, your reply was, "I'm here for the long haul, Ri." We smiled, and that was that. Thank you for loving me as I am!

Brett, thank you for your friendship, mentoring, and belief in me. I still laugh when I think about how God orchestrated our whole meeting and how you became my "agent." (You are my agent, aren't you?) I value your trust and guidance and am grateful for you!

Lisa, thank you for being an amazing listener! My goodness, I have rambled hours and hours of stories to you, six years' worth to be exact. I am certain many were out of order and made no sense, yet you kept listening and asking questions until we figured it out. There is absolutely no way to say thank you enough for all the hours you have put in on this book. Thank you! Thank you!

I feel like I can never say thank you enough. I could write a whole book of thank-yous, but I'm afraid I've already used up my word allotment. I am continually blessed by the people in my life who believe in the calling the Lord has placed in me. Not only do they believe in me, but they are always encouraging and ready to help at a moment's notice. Thank you to every person who picked up this book and read it. Thank you to my friends and family who have been by my side every step of the way and are willing to sort school supplies or volunteer at the store anytime they are in Branson or anytime we ask for a little extra help. Thank you to the people who come into the thrift store and tell me what a wonderful thing it is we're doing. I am so thankful for that encouragement each day. Thank you to the many churches that are always supporting us, not only financially but also in prayer.

## FROM LISA

For me, this project began with an urgent care visit for one child, ended with an urgent care visit for the other, and had a cross-country move (not to mention two random broken bones) sandwiched between. That probably accounts for my mental state across the whole duration of the work. Never have I felt more at a loss about how to complete a project, and never have I been more grateful for the kindness of others in the midst of it.

Riley, you have been generous and gracious, not to mention patient, bold, and brave, through every interview and every publishing phase. The tenacity of your faith is a stunning thing to see, and it has been personally inspiring to me. Helping to introduce readers to you and to the God we serve is a privilege.

Carolyn, you have proven yourself to have more patience and gentleness than any editor should ever have to. Had I known how much I would turn into a complete wreck of a person while working on this manuscript, I certainly wouldn't have dared sign on in the first place.

Greg, you have been fabulous as ever and as always. I had no idea how much I needed an agent like you when I submitted that first manuscript years ago. You combine no-nonsense with advocacy in a way that is brilliant. Nothing else could be a better professional match for me.

Hannah and Kelly, thank you for cleaning my house and Ziplocking everything so I could write even during our big move—there's no better friend than the one who's willing to help keep your junk drawer organized. Krista, Stacy, Chloe, and Trisha, thank you for being the friends and childcare providers my kids and I are happy to see every time. Matt, thanks for driving Chloe in the mornings so often. Dennis and Denise, Chuckie and John, John and Leizl, thanks for letting us crash with you at various times during our move, and thanks for not being annoyed when I stole away to work, again and again. Mom and Dad (both sets), thanks for all your encouragement and especially for your visits, which were delightful and gave incredible relief.

Celia and Benson, you're still too little to understand how much it means to me that you've been so endlessly patient and sweet. Let's go get that ice cream.

Nathan, you have put up with far more than we both thought you would need to on this one. Thanks for being my housekeeper, assistant, short-order cook, launderer, and therapist in turn, on top of all your usual impressive accomplishments. You are the best a girl could ask for, no question.

A friend of mine once told me, "God's past faithfulness predicts his future faithfulness." There were plenty of times when I couldn't understand what God was up to, putting me on this project. I felt too inadequate and messy to even begin. But a completed manuscript is proof yet again: he has been astonishingly faithful to me.

# *Notes*

## Chapter 28: Shattered Dreams

1. "Kenya Travel Warning," *US Passports and International Travel*, November 10, 2015, http://travel.state.gov/content/passports/english/alertswarnings/kenya-travel-warning.html.
2. "Kenya's Nairobi Hit by Twin Bomb Blasts in Gikomba Market," *BBC News Online*, May 16, 2014, http://www.bbc.com/news/world-africa-27443474.